WALKING

NIDDERDALE
& RIPON

HILLSIDE GUIDES - ACROSS THE NORTH

•JOURNEY OF THE AIRE   •JOURNEY OF THE WHARFE

Long Distance Walks
•COAST TO COAST WALK   •DALES WAY   •CUMBRIA WAY
•WESTMORLAND WAY   •FURNESS WAY   •NIDDERDALE WAY
•BRONTE WAY   •CALDERDALE WAY   •PENDLE WAY

Circular Walks - Yorkshire Dales
•East: NIDDERDALE & RIPON •West: THREE PEAKS & HOWGILL FELLS
•WHARFEDALE   •MALHAMDALE   •WENSLEYDALE   •SWALEDALE

Circular Walks - Lancashire/North West
•BOWLAND   •PENDLE & THE RIBBLE   •LUNESDALE
•WEST PENNINE MOORS   •ARNSIDE & SILVERDALE

Circular Walks - North Pennines
•EDEN VALLEY   •ALSTON & ALLENDALE

Circular Walks - Mid Yorkshire
•HARROGATE & WHARFE VALLEY   •HOWARDIAN HILLS

Circular Walks - South Pennines
•ILKLEY MOOR   •BRONTE COUNTRY   •CALDERDALE

Hillwalking - Lake District
•LAKELAND FELLS - SOUTH   •LAKELAND FELLS - EAST
•LAKELAND FELLS - NORTH   •LAKELAND FELLS - WEST

Short Scenic Walks - Yorkshire Dales
•UPPER WHARFEDALE   •LOWER WHARFEDALE   •MALHAMDALE
•UPPER WENSLEYDALE   •LOWER WENSLEYDALE   •SWALEDALE
•NIDDERDALE   •SEDBERGH & DENTDALE
•RIBBLESDALE   •INGLETON & WESTERN DALES

Short Scenic Walks - Northern England
•HARROGATE & KNARESBOROUGH   •ILKLEY & WASHBURN VALLEY
•AIRE VALLEY   •AMBLESIDE & LANGDALE   •AROUND PENDLE
•RIBBLE VALLEY   •HAWORTH   •HEBDEN BRIDGE   •BOWLAND

*Send for a detailed current catalogue and price list
and also visit www.hillsidepublications.co.uk*

WALKING in YORKSHIRE

——

NIDDERDALE
& RIPON

Paul Hannon

——

Hillside

HILLSIDE PUBLICATIONS

20 Wheathead Crescent
Keighley
West Yorkshire
BD22 6LX

First published in this format 2014
Previously published as *Nidderdale* (2006)
and *Ripon & Lower Wensleydale* (2007)

© Paul Hannon 2014   ISBN 978-1-907626-12-8

Cover illustrations: West Tanfield; Gouthwaite Reservoir
Back cover: Brimham Rocks; Page One: River Nidd at Hampsthwaite
Page Three: Lacon Cross; Above: Wath Bridge; Opposite: Yorke's Folly
(Paul Hannon/Yorkshire Photo Library)

The sketch maps are based on 1947 Ordnance Survey One-Inch maps

Printed in China on behalf of Latitude Press

CONTENTS

INTRODUCTION.....................6

THE WALKS (mileage in brackets)
 1 Ripley Landscapes (7)..........10
 2 Around Birstwith (5³4)..........14
 3 The Nidd at Darley (5¹4).......17
 4 Brimham Rocks (5)..............20
 5 Yorke's Folly (6¹4).............24
 6 Panorama Walk (5).............27
 7 Tramway to Wath (5)..........30
 8 Merryfield Mines (6¹2)..........33
 9 Fountains Earth Moor (8¹4)....36
10 Dale Edge (9)....................39
11 Around Ramsgill (5¹2)..........42
12 How Stean Gorge (4¹4)........46
13 Goyden Pot (7)..................50
14 Nidd Head Reservoirs (6)......54
15 Slipstone Crags (7)..............57
16 Ilton Moor (9)....................60
17 River Burn (7)...................64
18 West Tanfield (7)...............68
19 Hackfall Woods (6¹2)...........72
20 Laver Country (8)...............76
21 Fountains Abbey (5)...........80
22 Eavestone Lake (5).............84
23 Ripon's Rivers (5¹4)............87
24 Ripon Canal (6).................90
25 Copgrove (6¹2)..................93

INDEX................................96

INTRODUCTION

Nidderdale is probably least known of the major valleys of the Yorkshire Dales, but those who think the attractions of the Dales end at the National Park boundary will miss out on the multitude of delights within these pages.

Most of this guide falls within the bounds of the Nidderdale Area of Outstanding Natural Beauty, some 233 square miles that was designated in 1994. This fully merited if belated recognition of the scenic qualities of this landscape goes some way to offsetting its exclusion from the national park. The area of this guide divides into two equal neighbourhoods, namely Nidderdale itself, and across its eastern watershed, a series of delightful side valleys falling to the lower reaches of the River Ure, based on Ripon and Masham.

Above the hub of Pateley Bridge, Nidderdale is a well defined typical upper Dales valley, its narrow floor flanked by increasingly steep moorland heights. Sleepy villages and sheep farms straggle out towards the reservoirs of Scar House and Angram that occupy a bleak dalehead setting beneath the mighty Great Whernside: somewhat older is the more natural-looking Gouthwaite Reservoir. Other features of the upper dale include the natural highlights of Goyden Pot and How Stean Gorge, while the sturdy settlements of Middlesmoor, Ramsgill, Lofthouse and Wath present a precious, timeless quality.

Downstream from Pateley Bridge the more pastoral Nidd Valley sweeps gracefully through a landscape of fields and woodland to terminate at Ripley. This gateway village boasts unique character, while its neighbours Hampsthwaite, Birstwith and Dacre Banks are all a delight. Even below Pateley there remain glorious pockets of gritstone moorland, most famously at Brimham Rocks and Guise Cliff.

Aside from its natural rockscapes and man-made lakes, Nidderdale boasts two other outstanding aspects - heather and trees. The valley is little short of lavished with attractive woodland, while heather moors reach almost endlessly over sweeping horizons. Before passing to the wealthy abbeys of Fountains and Byland, Nidderdale was a Royal hunting chase, and today much of this vast moorland is managed as grouse shooting country.

Nidderdale's eastern skylines reach across broad moorlands to a delectable series of short valleys falling to the River Ure. Within

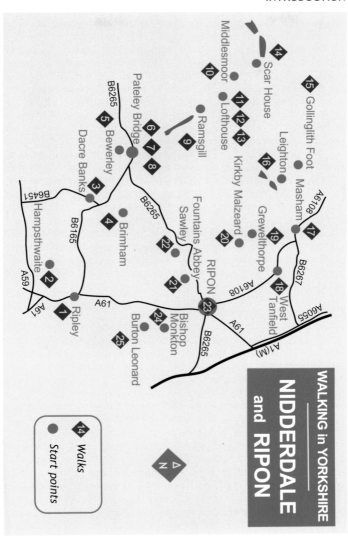

WALKING in YORKSHIRE
NIDDERDALE
and RIPON

14 Walks
● Start points

7

this graceful curve the Ure embraces an upland scene drained by the tributary rivers Burn, Laver and Skell. This area incorporates one of the brightest jewels in the Yorkshire crown, Fountains Abbey and the adjacent water gardens and deer park of Studley Royal. Having left the national park near Middleham, the Ure still has a wealth of absorbing countryside to travel through, leading by way of Masham to the city of Ripon. This tiny cathedral city is the focal point of the lower Ure, well sited for the A1(M) and offering all manner of attractions and accommodation: its glory is its imposing cathedral, a major landmark for many miles around.

The Ure's banks also support the charming old market town of Masham, based around a massive square and home to two celebrated breweries. Delightful villages abound, including Sawley and Fearby, West Tanfield and Kirkby Malzeard, featuring old stone cottages stood back from spacious greens. The area's wilder features are spread around the the extensive Ilton and Agra Moors. Here you will discover the hugely characterful gritstone outcrops of Slipstone Crags and White Lodge Crags, along with moorland boundary stones hidden in the heather. You will also encounter some remarkable curiosities such as the Druid's Temple at Ilton and the follies of Hackfall Woods at Grewelthorpe.

Access to the countryside

The majority of walks are on public rights of way with no access restrictions, or long-established access areas and paths. A handful also take advantage of the 2004 implementation of Right to Roam: any walks making use of Open Country are noted as such in their introduction, though on most days of the year you are free to walk responsibly over these wonderfully invigorating landscapes. Of the restrictions that do pertain, the two most notable are that dogs are normally banned from grouse moors (other than on rights of way); and that the areas can be closed to walkers for up to 28 days each year, subject to advance notice. The most likely times will be from the 'Glorious Twelfth', the start of the grouse shooting season in August, though weekends should largely be unaffected. Further information can be obtained from the Countryside Agency, and ideally from information centres. Finally, bear in mind that in spring, avoiding tramping over open country away from paths would help safeguard the crucial period for vulnerable ground-nesting birds.

Though bus services within the area are generally limited, availability, if any, is mentioned in the introduction to each walk. The nearest railway stations are at Harrogate and Northallerton.

Using the guide

The walks range from 4½ to 9 miles, with the average distance being around 6¼ miles. Each walk is self-contained, with essential information being followed by a concise route description and a simple map. Dovetailed in between are snippets of information on features along the way: these are placed in *italics* to ensure that the all important route details are easier to locate. Start point postcodes are a rough guide only for those with 'satnav': grid references are more precise!

The sketch maps serve to identify the location of the routes rather than the fine detail, and whilst the description should be sufficient to guide you around, the appropriate Ordnance Survey map is recommended. To gain the most from a walk, the detail of a 1:25,000 scale Explorer map is unsurpassed. It also gives the option to vary walks as desired, giving a much improved picture of your surroundings and the availability of any linking paths for shortening or lengthening walks. Four maps cover all the walks:

- *Explorer 298 - Nidderdale (this covers 18 of the 25 walks)*
- *Explorer 299 - Ripon & Boroughbridge*
- *Explorer 302 - Northallerton & Thirsk*
- *Explorer OL30 - Yorkshire Dales North/Central*

Also very useful for planning is Landranger map 99, with small parts also featuring on sheets 98 and 104.

Useful contacts

Nidderdale Area of Outstanding Natural Beauty
The Old Workhouse, King Street, Pateley Bridge HG3 5LE
• 01423-712950   www.nidderdaleaonb.org.uk

Information Centres
Minster Road **Ripon** HG4 1QT • 0845-3890178
1 Hall Square **Boroughbridge** YO51 9AN • 01423-322956
Royal Baths, Crescent Road **Harrogate** HG1 2RR • 0845-3893223
18 High Street **Pateley Bridge** HG3 5AW • 0845-3890179
7 Little Market Place **Masham** HG4 4DY • 01765-680200
Open Access • 0845-100 3298   www.countrysideaccess.gov.uk

RIPLEY LANDSCAPES

From the unique charm of Ripley, a string of neat villages are linked by way of pleasant fieldpaths

START Ripley (SE 284605; HG3 3AY)

DISTANCE 7 miles (11km)

ORDNANCE SURVEY 1:25,000 MAP Explorer 298 - Nidderdale

ACCESS Start from the market cross in the village centre. Car park at the entrance. Harrogate-Ripon bus.

Ripley exudes character and breathes history. It was a market town in 1357, and has been the manorial seat of the Ingilby family since before that. Nothing here is without interest, though the castle is the major attraction. First sighting is the imposing gatehouse, dating from the early 15th century. Through its great arch are spacious lawns and a courtyard. The castle itself was largely rebuilt in 1555, and much enlarged in 1780, though the old tower is less than a century after the gatehouse. After the battle of Marston Moor this Royalist castle supposedly received a visit from Oliver Cromwell, while his troops shot Royalist prisoners they had brought to the village. The lakes and deer park were laid out by Capability Brown, these magnificent grounds being open daily throughout the year. The castle is also open at various times during the year, and daily in high summer. It is well worth a visit for both its splendid interior and the contents within.

The village is an attraction in its own right, with farm museum, shops and tearoom. This classic estate village was rebuilt by Sir William Amcotts Ingilby in 1827, based on a French village of Alsace Lorraine - note the town hall named Hotel de Ville. All Saints' church dates from 1400, and the Ingilby chapel has life-size effigies of Sir Thomas and Lady Ingilby from around 1370. In its yard is a pre-Reformation weeping cross: far from comfortably positioned sockets cater for the knees of four penitent souls. The medieval market cross has stocks alongside, behind which - after a 70-year lapse - a licensed house was restored to the village in 1990: inevitably, the Boars Head features on the Ingilby crest.

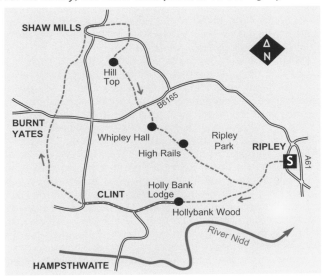

From the square follow the side road between the church and the castle, losing its surface to drop down to cross Ripley Beck before rising away outside the park wall, with a choice of paths. Look back for a glimpse of the castle above the lake. This enclosed track of Hollybank Lane rises to meet a broader track at a corner of the park wall at Sadler Carr. *In the trees in front is the site of a medieval manor house, partly enclosed by a defensive moat. This*

11

is clearly discerned from a little path venturing in just a few strides ahead. Keep left a short way, and when the broader track swings down to the left keep straight on a more inviting bridle-track. This runs beneath fine oaks into Hollybank Wood. *These glorious woodlands are perhaps at their finest when carpeted with bluebells.*

Emerging at Holly Bank Lodge, advance along the narrow road, rising to meet the road in Clint. Keep straight on Clint Bank Lane, passing Clint Cross. *Ancient stone tiers support a hollowed cross base, and some old stocks stand alongside. The cross bears the inscription 'Palliser the Tailor', companion to an equally intriguing one on Tang Beck bridge at the start of WALK 2.* Enjoying wide views over the valley, including down into Hampsthwaite, the road with its broad verge leads to a T-junction at the end.

Cross to a gate and across the field past the isolated remains of Clint Hall. *A forlorn little ruin is all that remains of this seat of Sir William Beckwith.* Beyond it is a gate in a wall, from where advance with the wall and then fence to a tiny tree-lined stream. Over a stile, don't cross the trickle but take a stile to the right, and an enclosed path rises parallel. Just short of the wood ahead, cross to a small gate on the left and resume up the other side. At the field top Burnt Yates' church spire appears just ahead. Remain on the fieldside to a gate where a track continues on to a tapering conclusion. Through the stile an access road then winds out onto the B6165 through Burnt Yates. *On the left is the 19th century church alongside the former Bay Horse pub. The New Inn survives at a crossroads a quarter-mile to the right. Across the road to the left is the characterful-looking school, built and endowed in 1760 by Admiral Robert Long.*

Just to the right a walled cart track drops away opposite. *Ahead, Bishop Thornton sits on its ridge across this side valley of Thornton Beck.* At farm buildings at the bottom continue down to a gate, and descend the fieldside to a stile in the very corner. Continue down the next fieldside, using stiles to cross an access road, and pass left of ramshackle outbuildings to a crumbling wall-stile. Resume again, and when the fence turns off, go straight down to a stile. This reveals Shaw Mills a field's-length away. Drop down the last colourful hedgeside to a small gate onto an access road, and turn right onto the road and bridge at the edge of the village. *Shaw Mills grew as housing for workers at nearby High Mill, and takes its name from mill-owner Robert Shaw. The Nelson Arms fell a little short of two centuries of serving ale, and by 1998 had closed. The environs of the bridge make a fine floral display with old steps down to Thornton Beck, so you'll just have to drink that in.*

Cross the bridge and follow the road to the village edge. *On the left is a former Methodist Church and School of 1904.* At the bend a short path on the right runs to a stile, with a short snicket to a stile into a field. Head away, bearing right to join a wall leading to a gate. Advance further, to a path crossroads where from a stile on the right drop to a footbridge on tree-lined Thornton Beck. Across, rise up the field to a stile onto a road. Opposite, an enclosed path makes a long, slanting ascent up a fieldside to ultimately reach a stile at the very top. *Look back over Shaw Mills in its broad valley.*

Advance to the farm buildings at Hill Top, passing between them to the yard. Go left onto the drive which leads out to a sharp bend by another house. Here, as it becomes surfaced, take a stile in front and bear gently left to a wall-stile opposite. Now follow the right-hand wall through two fields to a stile back onto the B6165. Go left briefly on the footway and cross to a gate opposite. Follow the hedge away, and halfway along pass through a gap in it.

Now bear left to a protruding hedge corner in front of the buildings at Whipley Hall, and follow the hedge to the gate just beyond.

Joining an access road by the buildings, turn left to a surfaced fork, and bear right. This passes High Rails Farm to meet the estate wall. Remain on this same way past the attractive Park Lodge. As a firmer track it shadows the park wall back down to meet the outward route at Sadler Carr. Turn left back into Ripley.

Ripley Cross and stocks

AROUND BIRSTWITH

Delightful beckside, parkland, riverbank and woodland walking on the southern slopes of the Nidd Valley

START *Hampsthwaite (SE 259587; HG3 2EU)*

DISTANCE *5³⁄₄ miles (9km)*

ORDNANCE SURVEY 1:25,000 MAP *Explorer 298 - Nidderdale*

ACCESS *Start from the village centre. Roadside parking. Harrogate-Pateley Bridge bus.*

Hampsthwaite is a sizeable village whose focal point is an attractive green. On it stands the old village pump, while close by are the Joiners Arms, Post office and shop. Hampsthwaite marked an important river crossing for the Romans on their road from Ilkley to Aldborough: a graceful old bridge now soars across the Nidd here. The parish church is visited at the end of the walk.

From the green take the Birstwith road updale, immediately out of the village. After a few minutes it narrows to bridge Tang Beck. *Note the intriguing inscription on the south side, 'Palliser the Hatter', a twin of the 'Tailor' seen on Clint Cross (WALK 1).* Immediately over, take a stile on the left and head away upstream along this broad, shallow valley floor. A splendid section traces the beck tightly past Gormires Wood across it, through several fields to ultimately emerge onto a back road. Cross straight over to a wall-stile and resume. This time the valley takes some shape, and the way slants up the bank to a gap-stile ahead. Advance to the next stile in a hedge, and then follow a hedge away to a corner gate. Here an enclosed grassy way runs on to join a drive at a house, which leads out onto a road at a nice cottage and triangular green.

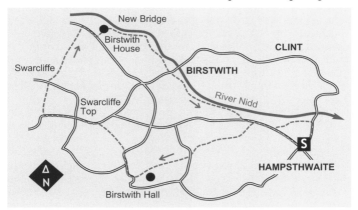

Turn right steadily uphill, and just beyond a junction leave the road where it bends right. A wall-stile in the corner sends you directly up the fieldside, rising to a ladder-stile in the very corner. Continue rising the same way to a wall-stile at the top corner onto another road. Turn left and continue gently rising, through a cross-roads at Swarcliffe Top and up a little further until beyond several nice cottages the road finally levels out. At the walk's high point, at a bend, take a stile on the right and cross to the opposite corner of the field. *From this high vantage point savour extensive views over a great curve of the valley to the higher moors, right up over Guise Cliff to Great and Little Whernsides on the distant skyline.*

Through the gate turn right with the wall, to a gate at the end where an enclosed green way heads off. This descends to send you straight on through a wall-stile in front. Now a thin path descends the side of a scrubby gorse enclosure, being deflected left at the bottom to a gap by a gate onto a back road at Swarcliffe. Turn briefly right to a farm, then go left down a walled driveway. By the lone house at the bottom go straight on down a path into trees, a super descent of the woodside with fine views ahead over the

Birstwith neighbourhood. Towards the bottom descend a fieldside onto the valley road - the Nidd is just below. Turn right for a short while, a gentle rise with a decent verge. *There is barely a dwelling in sight amid the valley's outstanding wooded scenery.* At a bend escape down a narrow lane on the left by Birstwith House. *With a farm on the right, note the lovely house of 1688 with mullioned windows on the left.* From the gate at the bottom a track continues down, and a path takes over to approach the river. Though the route takes a stile on the right, first advance a few steps further to admire the beautiful arch of New Bridge. *Dating from around 1615, it was on a Skipton-Ripon packhorse route, but was demolished in 1822 and rebuilt 25 yards downstream.*

Back at the stile turn downstream for a delightful section, soon cutting out a bend of the river as it shadows a hedge outside a cricket pitch. *Ahead is the feeds mill at Birstwith, and to the right the rather more elegant tall spire of Birstwith church.* At the end the river is rejoined as you trace the edge of sports fields to emerge onto the road in Birstwith. A mill-race shadows the route out to the road from a wide weir on the Nidd. *Just to the left the river bridge leads to the Old Station Inn, while Birstwith's attractive corners are along to the right, including the popular Post office/shop.*

Cross straight over the road towards the feeds mill yard. The path has been diverted to the left of the mill, so after re-crossing the mill-race on a footbridge, shadow the perimeter fence around above the river. At the end double back right with the fence, along to a kissing-gate back onto the original line of the path. Here turn left on a wallside path outside the trees, and from a stile at the end, rejoin the riverbank. This leads pleasantly downstream again, now for a considerable ramble. The point of leaving is at a bridle-gate back into a field, with a large barn up to the right: bear up to it, where a kissing-gate deposits you back onto the road.

Bear left along the road for Hampsthwaite, varying the entry into the village just after the church tower appears ahead. At a bend at the village sign, bear left on a gem of a part-flagged, leafy byway (the old churchgoers' way from Birstwith) to emerge into the churchyard. *The church of St Thomas a'Becket was much restored by the Victorians, but the tower is a good 500 years old.* A path runs along the front of the church and out onto the village street, with the village centre just to the right along Church Lane.

THE NIDD AT DARLEY

*An unbroken riverbank ramble from Dacre to beneath Darley,
followed by a sustained pull to the hilltop hamlet of Hartwith*

START *Dacre Banks (SE 196619; HG3 4EN)*

DISTANCE *5$\frac{1}{4}$ miles (8$\frac{1}{2}$km)*

ORDNANCE SURVEY 1:25,000 MAP *Explorer 298 - Nidderdale*

ACCESS *Start from the village centre.
Car park opposite the pub. Harrogate-Pateley Bridge bus.*

*Dacre Banks is a pleasant village with name and setting to
match, sat above the west bank of the Nidd. Across its green is the
welcoming Royal Oak pub: there is also a useful shop. The old
school served as a youth hostel for over half a century until 1987,
while Holy Trinity church stands closer to the river.* From the green
take a little lane between pub and car park, and quickly branch left
down into a yard. Drop down and along to the right near more
houses, and at the end take a gate on the left by an outhouse. Pass
through a gate and over a trickle, then cross to a gate ahead. From
here a thin path crosses to gain the riverbank path. Turn right and
settle down to an extended ramble alongside the tree-lined Nidd.

*During this first mile pause to look back at Low Hall's splendid
facade: some stones in this Tudor-style house are said to have
come from Fountains Abbey.* You soon encounter the former Nidd
Valley Railway alongside an old underpass. *The forlorn bridgework*

is a sad reminder of a typical rural branch line. Opened in 1862 largely to serve industry in the dale, it ran from near Harrogate to Pateley Bridge. The single-track line finally succumbed in 1964, having already been closed to passengers 13 years earlier.

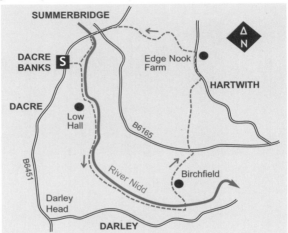

With the old rail embankment on the right, the path soon enjoys greater freedom as it ambles on past stepping-stones to cross a footbridge on inflowing Darley Beck. *Darley is seen up to the right, indeed a snicket runs up to it. The village spreads for a mile along the valley flank, with its Wellington pub at the western end above Darley Mill's retail delights. The village has a Post office/shop and a modest church, while a green bears stocks and is backed by attractive cottages.* The path runs along garden foots on the site of Darley's former railway station: a final open section leads to a tall footbridge on the river. *Immediately downstream is an old ford.*

Finally cross the river and a path runs briefly downstream before heading away along a fieldside. Two houses face you, White Oak to the left, and Birchfield Farm to the right. Through a bridle-gate at the end, advance straight on through two small enclosures between the buildings, out into a field at the back. Now bear left to a bridle-gate in the corner, onto the White Oak drive. Turn right up this cart track through Willie's Wood, absorbing the other drive then climbing as an enclosed way. At a lone house continue up the drive until just short of the top, where rise left to a gate onto the B6165. Cross to a better verge and turn briefly left, then escape through a gate on the right to follow an access track up to a farm.

Pass left of the buildings and bear left through a gate to another gate in a fence alongside a wall. Now head away along the wallside, over the brow. *Ahead are Hartwith's church and scattered houses.* Towards the end, bear right to a gate in line with the church. Advance up the field centre, and while the bridleway continues to a gate onto the road, opt to turn right past the churchyard wall to a small gate between houses and a snicket onto a road. *The 'centre' of the community of Hartwith features St Jude's 19th century church, with a bell-cote, and the village hall and old school along-side.* Turn left up to the bend, absorbing the direct bridleway route by the old vicarage, and continue up, still rising! At the top is Edge Nook Farm, immediately after which turn left on a grassy, walled cart track. *Views look over the big curve of the lower valley.*

The track runs a splendid course to arrive at a path crossroads. Turn left through the gate and a bracken-draped path heads off, soon dropping more appreciably through colourful surrounds, revealing Dacre Banks on the valley floor. At a bend keep to the main way slanting right, the left-hand wall now replaced by a wooded bank. *Note a spring with a stone trough at the foot of the wall on your right.* The path slants grandly down to a bridle-gate in the bottom corner alongside a covered reservoir. Advance to another gate just ahead, then slant left down the field edge to a bridle-gate at the bottom. A short, leafy enclosed way drops down to a bridle-gate onto the road at Hartwith Bank at the top of Summerbridge. Turn down the road to descend to the crossroads with the B6165 in the village centre.

This bustling little village features the Flying Dutchman pub, a Post office, other shops, tearoom and chip-shop. It grew to importance in 1825 when New York Mill was opened, to be joined by several more in the area's industrial heyday. Cross straight over and - noting a house with a sundial - down Dawson Bank to cross the bridge on the Nidd. *Here stands an extensive sawmills.* Either remain on the road to re-enter Dacre Banks, or turn downstream on the riverside path past the sports fields before leaving the river to retrace the opening steps back to the start.

BRIMHAM ROCKS

A beautiful, wooded side valley plays support to the weirdly sculpted rocks that are the pride of Nidderdale

START Brimham Rocks (SE 208645; HG3 4DW)

DISTANCE 5 miles (8km)

ORDNANCE SURVEY 1:25,000 MAP Explorer 298 - Nidderdale

ACCESS Start from the large National Trust car park at the main entrance. Harrogate-Pateley Bridge seasonal weekend bus.

Brimham Rocks are Nidderdale's top visitor attraction, and cannot fail to impress a first-time visitor. From the car park a broad carriageway leads directly to Brimham House. This gets the walk off to a proper start, saving the delights of the intervening wonderland for journey's end. *Otherwise, turn off from the car park information board where a well-made path heads into the heart of things: countless offshoots break off to discover hidden delights, eventually re-emerging near the house. Formerly the Rocks House, it was built in 1792 by Lord Grantley for his moor keeper, and now serves as a shop and information point, with the usual National Trust aromas and adjacent refreshments. The rocks form an extensive collection of millstone grit outcrops, sculpted into wonderfully bizarre shapes by the process of millions of years of Yorkshire weather. Randomly scattered about the moor, they form the ultimate natural playground, both for playful children and serious rock climbers.*

Leaving these opening attractions for a possible re-run at the end, take the main path to the left of the house. Further splendid outcrops are encountered, including better known ones such as the Dancing Bear (immediately) and Idol Rock. Beyond the last rocks the firm path loops back to the right: here leave it by a narrow green path which maintains the northerly aim above the edge of the wood to the left. Further, it drops down, at times in a groove, onto a moor-edge farm drive. Double back left on this rough road, passing through woods to approach Brimham Rocks Farm (High North Pasture Farm on maps). Before it, however, leave it at the first gate on the right after the trees. Cross the field to a gate at the far end, then on again to a small gate in the far right corner, in front of North Pasture Farm. Enter the yard by another such gate, and leave by one on the left after the main buildings.

The Dancing Bear, Brimham

Bear right across the field, dropping slightly to locate a stile/gate in a fence by a tiny stream. Continue straight on a more open field to a gate at the head of a green way. Turn down it between enclosing walls, remaining on its pleasant course as it drops down to cross Fell Beck to reach a clutch of houses. *Most notable is the Old Hall on the right, with mullioned windows.* Their access track now rises onto the B6265. Descend left, with verges, to the hamlet of Fell Beck, passing the Half Moon pub.

Leave the road as it climbs away, directly opposite the Kirkby Malzeard branch, by way of a wall-stile on the left. Slant across to a gate above, then along the wallside to a small gate giving access to the buildings of Knoll Top. Go left after the house to a gate out of the yard, then swing right to a stile by a gate. Descend the wallside to another stile, then turn right above the beck to a gate. Of two little paths heading away through the trees take the upper one, a splendid stride well above the beck. A stile at the end puts you back into a field, which is crossed to drop to a hurdle-stile in the very corner. You are now back with the beck, with a weir just upstream. Across this stile you also cross the old mill-race. Turn right the few paces to meet a cart track at a crossroads of ways. Go left to cross the beck at a footbridge and cobbled ford. Remain in the wood by turning right on a gradually rising path. *Within the space of a few strides I watched deer grazing and startled a heron from under my nose here.*

On approaching a walled enclosure the path forks: keep right, the path continuing on the level through rampant hollies to leave the trees at a wall-stile below the isolated buildings of Low Wood. A path crosses to join a wider one descending from the left. The way remains level on a super green way to enter deep birchwoods. The path eventually merges into a broader one from the right. Advance (left) along this a short way to arrive beneath ruinous red-brick buildings, where the path doubles back down to the right. Fell Beck is re-crossed on a footbridge, and the path traces it downstream, a lengthy spell on the bank of an old mill-race. Further, with a millpond down to the left, the path passes beneath a massive retaining wall to emerge onto the minor road through Smelthouses.

Smelthouses is a charming hamlet in a setting to match. A rich assortment of graceful dwellings stand near the beck, where as early as the 14th century ore was brought from the lead mines for smelting by the monks of Fountains Abbey. These were joined by several flax mills, including possibly the earliest in the district, in

1798. It is now difficult to imagine that this sequestered spot was ever a hive of activity. The bridge wall is a good spot to linger.

Turn left over the bridge, and continue a short way up the road as far as a drive on the left at Wysing House. Already the Brimham Rocks skyline is evident. Just past the attractive range of buildings at Low Wood House, the track swings left. Here leave it by a gate on the right to follow a superb walled track, rising away ever steadily through the greenery. *This is a 'real' green byway, and a natural corridor: it is also a former Monks' trod, one of the cross-country trade routes radiating from Fountains Abbey.* Beyond the walls it rises by a wood then through more open surrounds: High Wood comes up for company, and the path soon leaves the trees, with typical Brimham outcrops now dominant on the left. Through a stile/gate at the top you emerge onto the moor road.

Heading left onto Brimham Moor, the drive back to the car park leaves the road to finish the walk, though an earlier fork sees a branch remain on the moor to escape the road a little earlier. Time to go exploring again!

Idol Rock, Brimham

YORKE'S FOLLY

An unbelievable mix of woodland, beck, moorland and rock scenery: unforgettable colours on a sunny September day

START *Bewerley (SE 157649; HG3 5HX)*

DISTANCE *6¼ miles (10km)*

ORDNANCE SURVEY 1:25,000 MAP *Explorer 298 - Nidderdale*

ACCESS *Start from the village centre. Roadside parking.*

Bewerley is a hugely attractive village with carefully tended gardens leading the eye to cosy cottages. From the green follow the road north, keeping left at an early fork where the Pateley road goes right. As the road climbs out, within a couple of minutes take a stile on the left. Head up the field, through a collapsed wall to the top, there deflected right to a stile. Descend a wallside to enter Fishpond Wood by a kissing-gate. Take the main path heading into the heart of the wood alongside a tiny stream, which is crossed by a footbridge before reaching the shore of an ornamental lake.

Towards the end of the pond's bank a much broader path is met, turn right on it to swing round to a stile alongside a narrow road. Take care here as you actually join a driveway, whereas the road itself is just below. Turn right along the road, crossing Raven's Gill then spiralling steeply uphill. As Skrikes Wood ends on the left, take a gate and ascend steeply through bracken up the wallside outside the trees, with a sunken way materialising to your right.

After a stiff pull a gap in a cross-wall is reached: the true path is fifty paces to the right, where the old track rises to a hidden stile. Now in a field, slant right up to an outer wall corner, and resume up two fieldsides to a stile onto a farm road at Raven's Nest.

Go left just a few strides towards the house, but then turn right up a short-lived grassy way to a gate onto the bottom corner of heather-clad Low Moor. Rising away, your splendid green track is quickly joined by a firmer shooters' track, rising grandly with a fence along the edge of the moor. To the left across Raven's Gill, the two towers of Yorke's Folly await. 100 strides beyond a gate alongside

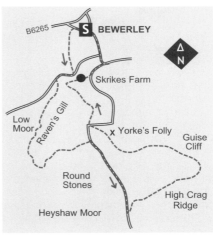

some massive boulders, after a wall takes over, turn left down a slim path. This descends into heather and bracken to gain the moist environs of Raven's Gill at a ruined sheepfold and waterfall. *Savour this idyllic spot from the grassy bank that overlooks the little falls.*

Across, a thin path slants left out of the gill, fading in the mix of heather and bracken on approaching a few outcrops. Just behind, a sturdy wall is joined at a substantial boundary stone. The simplest option here is to turn right, taking advantage of Open Access to trace a thin wallside path along to a gate onto the road. *A marginally more ambitious option rises straight up the moor to the small but very distinctive group of boulders at the Round Stones. Then simply continue straight up on a trod towards the brow, and forge on across the moor to meet a good shooters' track. Go left to a gate onto the road to rejoin the main route.*

Turn right up the road for a gentle rise to the brow of Heyshaw Moor. *This embraces a sweeping panorama over Nidderdale and beyond to the North York Moors.* After a gentler decline, leave by a stile/gate on the left. A very inviting broad path heads for the outcrops and Ordnance Survey column (1086ft/331m) on High Crag Ridge, awash in a colourful sea of bracken and heather. The path continues on towards a TV mast, keeping well to the left of an extensive - and extensively recolonised - former quarry.

Without entering the mast's confines go left on a path by an old wall, and after a stile in a fence, it crosses the wall to gain the exposed beginnings of Guise Cliff. Below is a wonderful panorama of the dale, seen as on a map beyond imposing rock architecture. *Children should NOT be near the edge, not only for the sheer drop (100 feet at its peak) but because there are also mischievous crevices. The views from the rocky edges are stupendous: the blanket of woodland below is so complete as to hide Guisecliff Tarn in its midst, though Gouthwaite Reservoir is seen up-dale.*

The path runs unerringly left along the crest, with tempting branches seeking out even more exposed situations. As the edge abates, the path runs on to a stile where the parallel fence turns to meet a wall. The wallside path continues on the moor edge to the waiting towers of Yorke's Folly, gained by a ladder-stile in the wall. *Highly prominent in many a Nidderdale scene, it was built 200 years ago by the Yorke family to provide employment. Supposed to resemble a Rhineland ruin, it probably does more so since one of the three original towers succumbed to a severe storm in 1893, rendering its local name of Three Stoops redundant.*

Beyond, the path leaves the wall to descend gradually through heather to the road on Nought Bank. From a gate behind the lay-by follow the main path down the moor. Passing through a kissing-gate it winds down into the top of Skrikes Wood, descending to a stile on the wood edge. Although this sends a short-cut path down the large field, better to remain in the wood on the path dropping left through trees. The path enjoys a grand descent to Raven's Gill at the bottom. Ignoring a footbridge to the left, turn downstream to leave the wood at a stile. Remain alongside the beck, passing below Skrikes Farm and then slanting up the bank to meet its drive just as it joins a back road. Turn left to a junction, then left over the bridge to follow a footway back into Bewerley. On the right is **Bewerley Grange Chapel**. *It was built as a grange by Marmaduke Huby, Abbot of Fountains, and was restored in 1965 within its peaceful grounds a world apart from Pateley just over the river.*

PANORAMA WALK

*A straightforward ramble, largely by the river but
beginning with a walk that lives up to its name*

START *Pateley Bridge (SE 157655; HG3 5JU)*

DISTANCE *5 miles (8km)*

ORDNANCE SURVEY 1:25,000 MAP *Explorer 298 - Nidderdale*

ACCESS *Start from the centre. Car parks. Bus from Harrogate.*

For a note on Pateley Bridge see page 33. From the bridge at
the foot of High Street head up the main thoroughfare, swinging
right at the top to quickly level out. After the Methodist Church an
urban path sign points up a flight of steps to the start of the
Panorama Walk. A steep, enclosed path climbs past an inscribed
stone above a well, with early views up-dale back over the church.
Beyond the cemetery entrance turn left onto a snicket running
along to the old church. *This offers wide views over Bewerley Moor
and Gouthwaite Reservoir beyond the gravestones. Hidden in trees
in high altitude seclusion, the roofless church of St Mary the Virgin
dates from the 14th century, with the tower added in the 17th. It
was abandoned in 1826 due to poor access, insufficient size and
repair costs, being replaced by St Cuthbert's church in the town.*

Resume by following the path up the churchyard a few strides
to locate a wooden kissing-gate in the wall on the right. A nice path
crosses a field to a gate, and on again to a stile at the end. A few

27

enclosed strides lead back onto the Panorama Walk. *Views back up the valley feature a distant Little Whernside.* Back on the main route the gradient eases and the narrow surfaced lane continues, enabling views to be appreciated effortlessly. Almost at once an iron gate admits to a viewing platform on a craggy knoll. *The Panorama Walk is, not surprisingly, a popular local promenade that lives up to its name. Probably the finest feature is the prospect of Guise Cliff directly across the valley, with Yorke's Folly silhouetted atop it.* On reaching the tidy hamlet of Knott, the way widens to drop down to the main road. *During this descent there are good views to Brimham Rocks bristling on the skyline to the left, while down-dale Summerbridge nestles amidst rich natural woodland.*

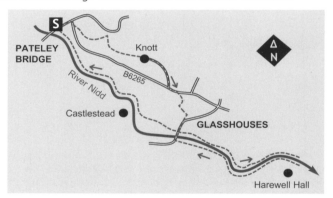

Two minutes along the footway to the left, cross to a kissing-gate just past a solitary dwelling. A flagged path leads down to a second field to descend to a rough lane on the edge of Glasshouses. Turn left a short way, then past an attractive terrace a very steep flagged snicket provides a short-cut towards the river. *Glasshouses village is an innocuous settlement based around a sloping green: dominant feature is the church spire, prominent in many a local scene. The village owes much of its existence to the Metcalfes, who erected housing and public buildings in the mid-19th century for workers in their great flax spinning mill.*

Rejoining the road, continue down past the former rail station and school to approach Glasshouses Bridge. *The walk returns to this point after a round trip of 2¹⁄₄ miles downstream, so if a short-cut is required, just pick up the route on the near bank and head upstream.* For the full route turn before the bridge into the mill-yard on the left, and leave it by bearing right immediately after the main building. This is not as per map, as there is no riverbank access between mill and river. *Glasshouses Mill dates proudly from 1874, boasting an imposing facade with an old clock and large bell. This substantial old mill now serves myriad operations, and its impressive riverside frontage is well seen from the return on the opposite bank.*

Passing down the far side of the mill a track descends to the river. A path largely clings to its bank, apart from a slant up to a wall-stile to run briefly above, while a little further a small corner is cut by way of stiles. The path passes under the remains of a viaduct to arrive at a wooden footbridge. *The former railway line to Pateley Bridge is much in evidence on this walk, and the forlorn viaduct's supports are a sad reminder of a typical rural branch line. The Nidd Valley Railway was opened in 1862 by the North Eastern Railway, largely to serve the dale's industry, and ran from near Harrogate to Pateley Bridge. Its single-track line finally succumbed in 1964, having been closed to passengers 13 years earlier.*

At the footbridge finally cross the river and turn upstream, clinging once more to the riverbank. *The farm up to the left is Harewell Hall, built by the influential Ingilby family in 1652.* After another section of viaduct the path passes through a nice wooded bank at a bend, then a sewage works before concluding in fine open surrounds as Glasshouses Mill appears. Glasshouses' singularly unglamorous bridge is quickly reached as a stile leads up onto the road. Cross the bridge and take the broad carriageway upstream for an infallible return to Pateley Bridge.

At once the drive is sandwiched between a mill-cut and a large millpond, now a haven for birdlife. *Rising high beyond the waters is the Guise Cliff skyline.* The river is regained at a weir. *Across it is the big house of Castlestead, erected in 1862 by the Metcalfes.* The Nidd is now traced upstream on an all-weather path. *A branch path runs to Harefield Hall, another large house, now devoted to serving hungry and thirsty public: the course of the railway line is also in evidence during the final attractive stages.* Path and river run together to re-enter the town alongside a linear car park.

TRAMWAY TO WATH

In delightful surroundings discover an inclined tramway that served a quarry, and a railway that helped build a reservoir

START *Pateley Bridge (SE 157655; HG3 5JU)*

DISTANCE *5 miles (8km)*

ORDNANCE SURVEY 1:25,000 MAP *Explorer 298 - Nidderdale*

ACCESS *Start from the centre. Car parks. Bus from Harrogate.*

For a note on Pateley Bridge see page 33. From the bridge at the foot of High Street, head up this main thoroughfare and go left on Church Street. *Along here you pass the playhouse, a former Salvation Army Citadel of 1859; the Oddfellows Hall; and the Nidderdale Museum.* Past St Cuthbert's church continue along Wath Road. After the last row of houses on the left it crosses a bridge: this is the immediately evident course of an inclined tramway that served the Scot Gate Ash Quarry high above. A stile gives access to the grassy incline, whose steep, unremitting course leads unfailingly to the old workings: pauses to savour the view back over the town are strongly recommended! The upper section becomes open and steeper alongside a wood, and from a stile at the top, only a minute's more climbing awaits, and you're there!

In these surprisingly extensive workings delphstone was won, a particularly strong form of millstone grit used as platforms and steps of important public buildings and works. The tramway was

30

built in 1873 by local entrepreneur George Metcalfe. It operated by steel ropes, with the loaded trucks descending a maximum 1 in 3 gradient as they assisted the empty ones to return to the top. The descent of 600 feet over a distance of 1000 yards ended at the railway yard at the bottom, where it was transferred to a standard gauge line for the next leg of its journey, out of the valley. It is within living memory that the quarry was a major source of employment.

At Wath

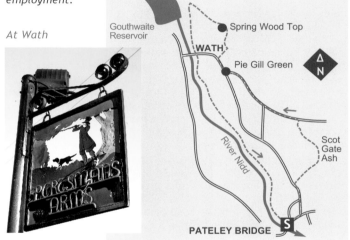

With the remains of the tramway winding house directly ahead, a track heads left, keeping close company with fence or wall. This superb path skirts the lower boundary of the quarry's heathery environs to emerge at the far end. *This stunning moment has sweeping views over the valley, with Great Whernside, Little Whernside and Middlesmoor seen beyond Gouthwaite Reservoir.* Head on through a gateway to then cross the field to a gate onto Wath Lane. This quiet byway leads downhill all the way back to the valley. *During this extended descent you can reap the rewards of the incline's pull and concentrate exclusively on the glorious panorama, major feature of which is the penetration of the upper dale by the finger-like Gouthwaite Reservoir beneath vast moorlands, while back down-dale the radomes of Menwith Hill intrude.*

At a junction continue straight ahead, descending to another junction at Pie Gill Green: turn right for a couple of minutes into Wath. *This tiny, unspoiled settlement boasts a wooded setting with numerous features of interest. First is the oddly-shaped Methodist chapel, dating from 1859 and still in use. At the bend beyond is an old mill, complete with bell, weather-vane, and workers' cottages, while the Sportsmans Arms features a fine individual sign.*

When the road turns sharp left towards the phone box and the hotel, leave by an access road right past a mullioned windowed cottage. The track climbs through woodland to a fork, keep left on past an old farm at Spring Wood Top. After a deep quarry hole it makes a gentle descent, with the waters of Gouthwaite Reservoir becoming more prominent ahead. You pass directly above the masonry dam, and a couple of fields later, leave the track by a gate on the left. *This is a good place to look over the extensive sheet of water, uncharacteristically natural-looking for a reservoir.*

A part-kerbed green track doubles back down the field to the edge of the dam wall. Here you encounter the grassy course of the old Nidd Valley Light Railway. *Opened in 1908 to convey material and men for construction of Angram dam at the dalehead, it also operated as a passenger line, but completion of Scar House dam in 1936 saw the end of its useful life.* From a small gate by the dam end, the path drops through trees to emerge into a pasture along-side the Nidd. Cross this to a stile, and then the last long pasture enjoys a charming riverside stroll to a stile onto the road at Wath Bridge. *Wath Bridge crosses the Nidd to meet the valley road, and is a lovely arched structure embowered in greenery. Originally a packhorse bridge it was widened in 1890, though is still small enough to recall the days when it served the monks of Fountains.*

Ignoring the bridge, take a simple footbridge opposite. From here a path crosses a field centre to a wall-stile, continuing on to meet the slightly embanked course of the old railway. From the next stile the line is followed for some distance to a point where the Nidd comes in alongside. Beyond a stile in this tree-shrouded setting the railway is forsaken for the river, whose tree-lined bank leads unerringly back to Pateley Bridge. Part way along, note the lively confluence at the arrival of Foster Beck. Reaching a weir the path becomes confined, and is deflected away to emerge between buildings onto Mill Lane adjacent to Pateley's graceful bridge.

MERRYFIELD MINES

A splendid all-weather excursion on well-defined
paths and tracks to an absorbing lead mining setting

START *Pateley Bridge (SE 157655; HG3 5JU)*

DISTANCE *6^{1}2 miles (10^{1}2km)*

ORDNANCE SURVEY 1:25,000 MAP Explorer 298 - Nidderdale

ACCESS *Start from the centre. Car parks. Bus from Harrogate.*

Pateley Bridge is a busy little town, the undisputed capital of
Nidderdale. It draws from far and wide: to locals it is the hub of
dale life, to visitors from further afield, the first stop. Within this
compact little town (more a village in size) are pubs and cafes, an
information centre, a riverside park, and innumerable individual
and absorbing shops, some hidden down inviting narrow alleys.
Within its little streets is a wealth of interest, certainly worth an
hour or two's observant pottering. The Nidderdale Museum carries
absorbing displays of life gone by, including Pateley's abandoned
industries of lead mining, quarrying and railways. Pateley Bridge
lost its rail service from Harrogate in 1964, though evidence is
encountered in a number of the walks. At Pateley, too, there is
always the river: the Nidd's banks carry paths in both directions,
and here, some decades ago, the author saw his first kingfisher.
Pateley Bridge is also home to the colourful Nidderdale Show, a
hugely popular event that takes place each September.

From the foot of the High Street, cross the bridge and turn immediately into the public park on the right. Remaining on the tree-lined riverbank, the embanked, initially surfaced path leads past the first caravan site of the day before gaining open fields. In the second of these the path cuts the corner at Foster Beck's entry into the Nidd, to a kissing-gate to the right of the prominent Brigg House Farm. Alongside a cottage a small footbridge crosses the beck, now followed upstream to another kissing-gate before crossing to another onto the Heathfield road junction at Corn Close.

Turn left, briefly, along the road down-dale to the Bridge Inn. *This recent pub conversion replaced the neighbouring Watermill Inn. The original pub occupied the former flax mill that operated as a ropemakers into the 1960s. Its spell as a pub saw it as a renowned folk venue, and restoration of the waterwheel made it an attraction in its own right. With the building now private apartments, the 35ft diameter wheel is well seen from the car park.*

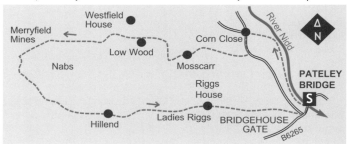

Continue a little further to a sharp bend, then turn right on a stony drive to Mosscarr Farm (a suburban bungalow), ignoring an uphill fork en route as the track opens out to run more pleasantly. Continuing behind island-like barns in the field centre, the track runs on to reach an idyllically sited cottage at Mosscarr Bottom. Just beyond are a footbridge and a ford in a wooded dell. Across, head briefly downstream before striking away up a splendid walled way to a track above Ashfold Side Beck. Turn right, descending to a bridge and a surfaced access road by a small caravan site.

This strip of tarmac is followed left, clusters of caravans now appearing with regularity. At a steep fork to Westfield House Farm, remain on the level road into another site. This threads its way through to finally shrug off the last caravan. This same track, a well-engineered mine road, leads all the way up this increasingly attractive and richly wooded side valley known as Merryfield Gill. Suddenly mine workings appear across the beck, and a path breaks off to drop to a big wooden bridge back across Ashfold Side Beck.

Merryfield Mines provide a marvellous insight into the dale's lead mining past, and Prosperous Smelt Mill is one of the major sites. The aim - allowing for cautious exploration - is to gain the far upper side of the workings. *Chief feature of note is the smelt mill, the large ruinous building in front, with a geared winding shaft forlornly in situ, and a peat store to its left; behind it is the line of an old flue, which rises steeply up the bank to terminate at the remains of a circular stone chimney in the heather.*

Turn downstream past the mill, then a green path slants up past the peat store, but quickly double back right to equally quickly reach the line of the flue: here a slim green path heads half-left through the heather to join a wide track. Turning right along it, the flue is again met just below the chimney ruin. Here the track fades to run along the foot of the main group of spoil heaps before you curve up to the top of the site, passing one last ruin and levelling out (now as a delectable green way) before reaching a gateway.

Beyond the gateway the track continues alongside a wall, soon joined by a firmer track at a junction just ahead. Ignoring a grassy branch left, continue down to cross shapely Brandstone Dub Bridge and head confidently away again. Coldstones Beck is crossed at a bend at Hillend, and the access road becomes surfaced. Several farms are passed on this narrow lane rising onto Ladies Riggs. *This lofty brow offers outstanding views both up-dale and down-dale.* About five minutes beyond Riggs House Farm the road enters a shroud of trees. Here leave through the few trees on the left to a stile in a corner. A grand stride follows the hedge downhill with Pateley Bridge directly ahead, its High Street appearing vertical.

Keeping the field boundaries on the right, the way ultimately becomes enclosed to drop down onto a back road at Bridgehouse Gate. *Just in front is the splendidly preserved former Metcalf's Brewery, taken over by John Smith's of Tadcaster in 1912: now converted to dwellings, it retains its typical small brewhouse appearance in a pleasing corner.* From here go right to the main road by the Royal Oak, then left back over the bridge into town.

FOUNTAINS EARTH MOOR

A bracing moorland ramble entirely free of navigational difficulties, tracing old trackways throughout its length

START *Ramsgill (SE 119709; HG3 5RL)*

DISTANCE *8¹4 miles (13km)*

ORDNANCE SURVEY 1:25,000 MAP *Explorer 298 - Nidderdale*

ACCESS *Start from the village centre. Roadside parking. Take care not to impinge on the green or block access, being aware of notices indicating the parts reserved for hotel patrons. Seasonal Sunday bus from Harrogate via Pateley Bridge.*

Ramsgill is a visually striking village on the banks of its own beck just short of its confluence with the Nidd. Prime feature is the spacious green, where attractive cottages and flowery gardens play support to the imposing ivy-clad hotel. Since extended, this former shooting lodge of the Yorke family still bears their name. A circular pinfold stands in front of the village hall. The solid-looking church of St Mary the Virgin was rebuilt in 1843, and looks out across the reedy head of Gouthwaite Reservoir. Ramsgill was an important grange of Byland Abbey, and at the rear of the church a solitary gable-end is all that remains of the monks' chapel.

From the green head north past the hotel on the Lofthouse road, but immediately after crossing Nidd Bridge turn right on the narrow lane to Bouthwaite. *En route, the course of the Nidd Valley Light Railway is crossed, adjacent to the old station house.* Passing a former Wesleyan chapel of 1890, the surfaced road ends at a junction of tracks in the centre of the hamlet. *Less than ten miles distant from this point, Fountains Abbey had an important grange here. It is interesting to note that while Nidderdale was in the grip of monastic landlords, it was shared by two abbeys that often had their differences: what they did agree on, by and large, was access on routes across Fountains' land to enable the Byland monks and workers to reach their Ramsgill grange and their possessions on the western side of the valley.*

Go straight on ahead to a gate, beyond which a stony track scales the hillside. *Halts reveal views back over much of the valley, including much of Gouthwaite Reservoir, while beyond Ramsgill the attractive side-valley of Ramsgill Beck tumbles from the moors. Nearer to hand, just above Lul Beck, a slate quarry operated into the early 20th century.* When the gradient eases the going underfoot

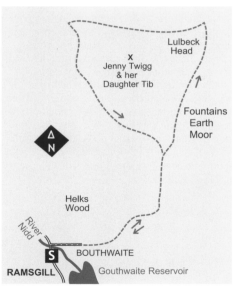

improves, rising all the way to Intake Gate and a junction at a wall corner. *The track continuing uphill is the old road to Kirkby Malzeard via Dallowgill.* Branch left to a second fork, to which you shall later return. *Once important highways that linked upper Nidderdale with its monastic landlords today serve only walkers, shooting parties and the occasional off-road biker.*

With a choice of gates opt for the right fork, a modern shooters' way overlaying a historic track rising gently through the heather of Fountains Earth Moor. *The moor is named from its early owners Fountains Abbey: Sypeland Crags break the skyline across parallel Lul Beck.* Higher up the track, beyond a gate, an inscribed boundary stone is passed to reach a T-junction. *This is also marked by an old guidepost, the right branch being the old road that engages several more upland miles towards Kirkby Malzeard and Masham.* Go left to commence a level march. *By now the underestimated vastness of these big sweeping moors is fully appraised: the great upland stretching east is criss-crossed by old trackways without a motor road in evidence save for the Lofthouse-Masham strip of tarmac.*

At a stone shooting house, halt at the gate to identify Jenny Twigg and her Daughter Tib, two rock monoliths on the near sky-line. *Since the advent of Open Access, an appealing diversion might be undertaken to inspect these natural obelisks at close hand.* Resuming, another junction is reached: here go left, inevitably, again on a superb green road for the most part enclosed by walls. Less historic than its counterparts, this was made at the time of the enclosures. In due course it leads back to the outward track, and all that remains is the pleasurable task of retracing the opening two miles back down to Bouthwaite and Ramsgill.

Jenny Twigg and her Daughter Tib

DALE EDGE

*A breathtaking circuit of the upper reaches of Nidderdale,
on excellent paths and tracks with outrageous views*

START *Middlesmoor (SE 092742; HG3 5ST)*

DISTANCE *9 miles (14$\frac{1}{2}$km)*

ORDNANCE SURVEY 1:25,000 MAP *Explorer 298 - Nidderdale
or Explorer OL30 - Yorkshire Dales North/Central*

ACCESS *Start from the village centre. Car park at the top.
Seasonal Sunday bus from Harrogate via Pateley Bridge.*

At a very windswept near-thousand feet up, Middlesmoor is
*Nidderdale's first village. Its name accurately reflects its position
on a broad tongue between the valley of the Nidd and its major
tributary How Stean Beck. The homely Crown Inn occupies an
attractive corner across from the old school. An intricate little
network of alleyways wind between sturdy gritstone cottages with
flowery gardens to the church, visited at the end of the walk.*

From the car park turn right up In Moor Lane, which at once
downgrades to a rough track. This wide, stony way leads unceasingly
but gradually upwards. *This route is the old road from Middlesmoor
to Coverdale by way of the Lodge: its approach to the Lodge was
drowned by the reservoir, and its purpose further diminished by
construction of the road to the dams on the bed of the old railway.*
The firmer track quickly turns left through a gate, but your way

39

remains on the walled lane, now a little rougher but more characterful. *Big views look west over the moors to Great and Little Whernsides and the Stean valley.* Eventually the way levels out on the moor-top of Rain Stang. Beyond a gate it finally runs free, and quickly starts a steeper descent towards Scar House Reservoir. *Ahead is a great sweep of Nidderdale's majestically wild upper reach, with Great Whernside and Little Whernside encircling the reservoirs. Opposite you is the extensive former Carle Fell Quarry.*

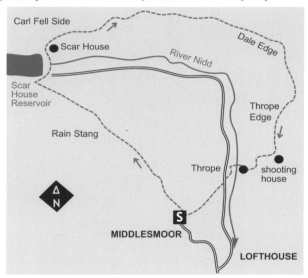

Descend to the water company road on the shore of Scar House Reservoir and turn right as far as the dam. *To the right is Scar House car park and WC.* Cross the dam and continue on the solid track which slants up to a rest-house. Just above it take the branch right, rising through a cross-tracks above the old reservoir keeper's house to a gate. A little beyond, marshy ground is encountered, but the path picks up to continue to another gate above the small Firth Plantation before dropping towards the deep cleft of Woo Gill. The track zigzags steeply down to the floor of the gill, then back out the other side crossing little Twizling Gill as it climbs away.

Emerging on the brow, remain on the firm track crossing to a gate, behind which is a shooting cabin. The grassier continuation immediately rises left to pick up a firmer, higher level track. Head right along this, commencing a near level trek around Dale Edge, remaining around the 1400ft/425m contour for a good two miles. With magnificent views and a superb track the whole way, instructions are superfluous as you contour round the large loop of the valley. *Long strides are the order of the day as the views along the length of the dale rank superlatives: a fine contrast is formed by the green of the valley at your feet and the dark outlines of rounded Meugher and the two Whernsides on the western skyline.*

At a crossroads of green ways the other track drops back down to the farms on The Edge, and its left branch crosses over towards Masham. Resuming through a slight rise, the way drops past a few rocks to reveal the unmistakable shooting house on Thrope Edge in a dip just ahead. Immediately before the shooting house an inviting green path zigzags down the bracken flank to a gate in the wall. *This super grassy way was built to provide easy access from the valley floor - the farmstead at Thrope is now directly below you.* The path heads more gently left before swinging sharp right on reaching a wood. Doubling back down through a few trees and down a fenceside, at the bottom bear left to a gate in the fence below. Now head straight down a field to a gate by a barn onto the track behind Thrope Farm. Turn right and then sharp left into the yard, going right of the farm to the drive, down to the river.

Crossing the Nidd, take a stile to head down the grassy bank. Halfway along the field, bear right through a gate in the wall, and continue across to a stile near the top corner. Go a few strides left on the road to another stile, and slant directly up several fields making use of some top quality wall-stiles. At a gate in a wall along the top, don't pass through but go left with the wall to pass through a pencil-thin wood. Now rise across a large field to a fence-stile above, with some of Middlesmoor's houses just above. Above this is a gate, through which curve up to a gate in the corner just above to re-enter the village near the church. *St Chad's was rebuilt in 1866 on an ancient foundation: a Saxon cross within is said to have been Chad's 7th century preaching cross. Its churchyard is also renowned as a foreground to a panorama down the length of the dale to Gouthwaite Reservoir and beyond.*

WALK
11 AROUND RAMSGILL

Upper Nidderdale's two valley floor villages are linked by fieldpaths on both sides of the dale: outstanding views

START *Lofthouse (SE 101735; HG3 5SA)*

DISTANCE *5$\frac{1}{2}$ miles (9km)*

ORDNANCE SURVEY 1:25,000 MAP *Explorer 298 - Nidderdale or Explorer OL30 - Yorkshire Dales North/Central*

ACCESS *Start from the village centre. Car park. Seasonal Sunday bus from Harrogate via Pateley Bridge.*

Lofthouse is a small, tidy village high above the river, focal point being the attractive corner which includes the homely Post office and an impressive water fountain which bears words worth reading. A house opposite the memorial institute bears a 1653 datestone. The Crown Hotel refreshes visitors, while the little school serves all the upper dale's youngsters. Alongside the school and WC on the bottom road is the former station house, which was the highest on the Nidd Valley Light Railway.

From the village centre fountain, take a gap in the corner of the square between cottages, and a firm path runs down a fieldside to a substantial footbridge on the Nidd. *Immediately upstream are the beautiful Nidd Falls.* Cross to emerge onto the Scar House road, straight over to a kissing-gate and on past the cricket pitch to another kissing-gate onto the bend of a road. Go right a few strides then fork left on the lesser How Stean Gorge branch. This runs past a car park to bridge How Stean Beck. Cross and turn left to Studfold Farm. *Once a small grange of Byland Abbey, an outdoor activity centre and a caravan site share the farming environs.*

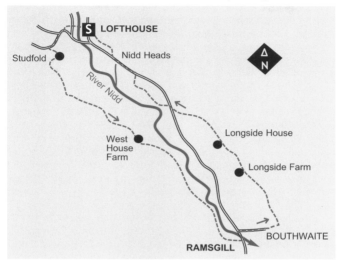

Turn sharp right up the steep, rough road to a line of cottages, after which take another walled track to the left. This runs on to cross Blayshaw Gill. *Peer over the bridge, downstream, to witness a superb narrow limestone ravine.* Emerging into a field the access track climbs to High Blayshaw Farm, but your way advances just as far as a barn. Now head straight along a more inviting, faint but embanked green track to a stile/gate combination repeated in the fields ahead. *The benefit of contouring the valley flanks gives this section panoramic views up-dale to Lofthouse, Middlesmoor and beyond.* The way rises slightly, then on past a barn to soon run as a firmer track through the fields to West House Farm.

Towards the farm the path is deflected left, using stiles to see a neat snicket between houses to emerge at the other end. Resume on a track heading away, dropping though a gate and down to the valley floor. Crossing a stone-slabbed tiny stream, the way at once

43

swings back up to a gate and along a field bottom. By now the track has become a faint grassy way. After one further gate, and with the river close by, advance on to merge into an access track from Grindstone Hill House, just above. This now leads unfailingly and very pleasantly along to Ramsgill, with the river at arm's-length down to the left. The village is entered by passing straight through a farmyard onto a small green. *For a note on Ramsgill see page 36.*

En route, the course of the Nidd Valley Light Railway is crossed at the old station house. Built to aid construction of the dale-head reservoirs, it also operated a passenger service from Pateley Bridge to Lofthouse but was dismantled after serving its main function. Passing a former Wesleyan chapel of 1890, the surfaced road ends at a track junction in the centre of the hamlet. *Less than ten miles distant at this point, Fountains Abbey had an important grange here. It is interesting to note that while Nidderdale was in the grip of monastic landlords, it was shared by two abbeys that often had their differences: what they did agree on, by and large, was access on routes across Fountains' land to enable the Byland monks and workers to reach their Ramsgill grange and their possessions on the western side of the dale.*

Advance a handful of strides further and take an enclosed access track bearing left between cottages to enter a farmyard. *On the left stands Bouthwaite Grange, a lovely old house with a 1673 datestone and mullioned windows.* From a gate at the end cross a wooden farm bridge on Lul Beck, then bear right to a gate in a recess just past a stile. An old way rises up the wood side, but at the top keep left with the wall, leading away from the wood. A faint path makes for an uncomplicated stroll on a delightful, direct course towards Longside Farm, several fields ahead. *This section enjoys views back down the valley to Gouthwaite Reservoir, with a substantial length of the old railway discernible in the fields. Middlesmoor is seen on its tongue of land between the Nidd and How Stean, with Little Whernside visible above the latter valley.*

From a gate just before the house at Longside Farm, slant right up a thin path to a gate in front of the large plantation. Turn left down a grassy track, merging with one from the house to run on to a gateway. Now bear right up another grass track towards Longside House. *From 1968 to 1983 this was a superbly sited youth hostel. The views from this neighbourhood are truly magnificent, both up and down the dale, and across to the moors above Ramsgill.* Passing between the rear of the house and the trees, a super path runs on the base of the wood to its far end. The way now crosses a pasture to a gate in the bottom corner, then drop to a redundant gate below. A field track then slants down to a stile by a gate in the corner below, where the invisible old railway leads out to the valley road: use a bridle-gate beyond the main gate.

Cross the road to a gate opposite and resume on the course of the old line. In the second field bear right off its embankment to a wall-stile by an old railway box, then continue to a stile just across the corner. Bear left to a gap between wall and trees at a small old quarry, and a track runs the final strides back to the road, with a stile just left of the gate. Turn left along the road for 250 paces to arrive at Nidd Heads. *Just over the wall the true river returns to daylight at a rocky door, after a lengthy subterranean spell since the environs of Goyden Pot further up-dale (see WALK 13). This is not the only resurgence, you've already passed a less obvious branch.* Lofthouse is now just two minutes ahead. Leave the road directly above Nidd Heads, a path rising to a stile into a field. Cross to a gap-stile in the wall across the field, and on a field bottom to a gateway. Part way along the next field you reach a channel dug to eradicate seepage: alongside where the water goes underground is a wall-stile. Cross the field to a stile back to the village centre.

Looking down on Ramsgill

HOW STEAN GORGE

A visit to How Stean Gorge is a trip to remember, and this memorable excursion adds attractions outside the ravine

START *Lofthouse (SE 101735; HG3 5SA)*

DISTANCE *4$\frac{1}{4}$ miles (7km)*

ORDNANCE SURVEY 1:25,000 MAP *Explorer 298 - Nidderdale or Explorer OL30 - Yorkshire Dales North/Central*

ACCESS *Start from the village centre. Car park. Further parking at either How Stean Gorge approach or Middlesmoor, also on the route. Seasonal Sunday bus from Harrogate via Pateley Bridge.*

Though not a necessary requisite, a torch will be of assistance if contemplating extra-curricular adventures, of which more shortly... For a note on Lofthouse, see page 42. From the village centre fountain take a gap in the corner of the square between cottages, and a firm path runs down a fieldside to a footbridge on the Nidd. *Immediately upstream are the beautiful Nidd Falls.* Cross to emerge onto the Scar House road, straight over to a kissing-gate and past the cricket pitch to another kissing-gate onto the bend of a road. Go right a few paces then fork left on the How Stean Gorge branch, which passes a car park to bridge How Stean Beck. *For a direct route to the gorge, remain on the road.* Cross and turn left to Studfold Farm. *Once a small grange of Byland Abbey, an outdoor activity centre and a caravan site share the farming environs.*

Turn sharp right up the steep, rough road to a line of cottages. Continue up, ignoring a branch to the left before levelling out. Immediately after a renovated farmhouse take a gate on the right, and a grassy track heads along the field bottoms to Whitbeck Farm. *En route enjoy super views over Lofthouse up to Thrope Edge and the moorland skyline, while Middlesmoor sits on its hill, and the valley of How Stean Beck, subject of your walk, is well revealed.*

A slim stile to the right accesses the drive, then go left up into the yard. Turn immediately right through a gate to drop to a foot-bridge, then resume along the field bottoms (via wall-stiles) to approach the next farmhouse. A few yards of flagged path lead to a small gate into its confines. Go straight ahead between house and barns, and out via a gap-stile into a field. Cross to another just ahead, then continue between a tiny stream and a wall to the bottom corner, where a single stone-slab bridge crosses a tiny beck to enter an attractive corner of Stean. *Here was another small grange of Byland Abbey. The immediate visitor attractions of this farming hamlet consist of a seat on a patch of green as you leave, but its famous gorge makes it a Yorkshire favourite.*

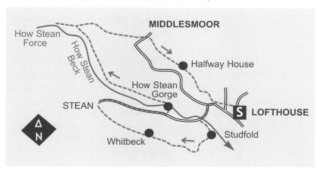

Turn downhill to leave by the access road. *Soon passed, at a bend, a squeezer-stile sends a footpath down to a footbridge over How Stean Beck - a useful short-cut if not visiting the gorge.* The road runs quickly along to the entrance to How Stean Gorge. *En route you pass good views into the ravine to whet your appetite, and also How Stean Tunnel on the right. If opting to explore the gorge, an entrance fee is payable at the cafe, which also has a gift*

shop. How Stean Gorge is a marvellous natural spectacle, a lime-stone ravine half a mile long and up to 80 feet deep. The rocks have been worn into dramatic contours by the timeless action of the swift-flowing water - deep, dark and wet caves abound.

The entire expedition is but a short one, the part downstream of the cafe being especially exciting as the pathway negotiates dramatically suspended bridges to guarded natural walkways through the rocks. Of perhaps greatest interest are How Stean Tunnel, near the walk's upper limit, and Tom Taylor's Chamber. Legend says it acquired its name from an outlaw who sought refuge here, but what is more certain is that Roman coins were unearthed in the 19th century. This 530ft cave runs from the gorge to the field behind the cafe, and even novice troglodytes might negotiate it with the aid of a torch (which can be hired).

On emerging, resume the walk by crossing the bridge to the car park field and locate a gate at the top left corner. Advance to a gate alongside a barn, then go left across several field-centres, using gates in walls beneath Hazel Close Farm, to meet a path descending from Middlesmoor at a fine wall-stile. Passing through, a path slants down the field to a bridle-gate above the steep wooded bank of the beck (with a footbridge just below). Don't pass through, but turn upstream to a wall-stile then a ladder-stile, from where a super little path drops gently down to the spritely beck. *These hugely colourful environs prove there is much more to How Stean Beck than its obvious main attraction.* On by a low limestone scar, at the end ignore a gate in front, and instead turn up a little nick in the scar to resume to a stile into a wooded bank hard by the beck. Through bracken and scattered trees a ruinous little stone shelter is passed, just beyond which the path makes a splendid slant up the wooded bank to a stile at the top corner.

While the route doubles back here from a stile just above, first advance a few strides, over a tiny trickle to a fork. Slant left back down into a large pasture, with How Stean Force visible just ahead. *The best viewpoint involves crossing an inflowing tributary to draw level with the Aysgarth-like falls.* From the waterfall retrace steps to the stile on the edge of the wood, where a second stile is located just a few paces above. From it climb briefly through bracken, then bear right to a stile at the foot of a length of wall. *This is a fine vantage point for the remote qualities of the How*

Stean valley. Follow a fence away to another wall-stile, then slant across a large field up to a gateway. *By now the view extends down-dale to bring in Gouthwaite Reservoir.* A track now runs to the farm ahead, but the path has been diverted along a pleasanter line by rising to the far corner. A wooded enclosure behind the farm leads down to emerge onto the road at the entrance to Middlesmoor, opposite the old Wesleyan chapel of 1899.

Middlesmoor is Nidderdale's first village, sharing its allegiance to the main dale with the major tributary that is the subject of this walk. Its name accurately describes this position, on a broad tongue 'twixt the two valleys. Just above, the Crown pub occupies an attractive corner. Leave the village by making for the church (see WALK 10), reached by way of a cobbled street on the left just after the phone box. To its right is a squeezer-stile, and a short snicket descends to a gate with seats alongside. A long flight of steps leads down into a field, from where a path maintains a straight line to Halfway House Farm. Go straight through the yard to a gate at the bottom, and head down the right side of a field to a stile. At the bottom swing left to a stile part way along, then bear left to a stile in the corner to emerge back onto the lay-by near to the start of the walk. Retrace your steps back over the footbridge, but first consider a tiny detour upstream to enjoy the shy charms of Nidd Falls.

How Stean Gorge

GOYDEN POT

An intimate exploration of the carefully tended upper valley, further enhanced by a cat-and-mouse game with the river

START *Lofthouse (SE 101735; HG3 5SA)*

DISTANCE *7 miles (11km)*

ORDNANCE SURVEY 1:25,000 MAP *Explorer 298 - Nidderdale or Explorer OL30 - Yorkshire Dales North/Central*

ACCESS *Start from the village centre. Car park. Seasonal Sunday bus from Harrogate via Pateley Bridge.*

For a note on Lofthouse see page 42. Leave the village by the Masham road which quickly starts to climb away from the houses. *This moorland road is the only motorable exit from the valley above Pateley Bridge, and even then it was only made fit for motor traffic in the 1960s.* Before the first bend, however, leave it by a grassy track along to the left. This is Thrope Lane, and beyond a gate it leads a splendid, unerring, mile-long course to Thrope Farm. *Thrope is the site of a small grange of Fountains Abbey.*

Remain on the track past the farm, and beyond a gate drop with a sunken way to the normally dry, stony bed of the Nidd. Continue upstream just a short distance to Dry Wath, an apt name for the ford you use to cross to a gate. A good path continues beyond, re-entering the wooded confines of the curving riverbed at a stile. *In the bed here, a manhole cover protects a vertical shaft* with metal steps: this is connected to the extensive Goyden Pot system. Just past it is a dark, stone-arched mine level. When a stile returns the path to the fields, it rises to join the drive to Limley Farm. *This attractive grouping is on the site of another old grange, this time of Byland Abbey.*

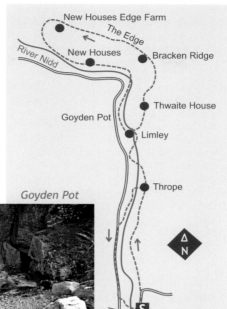

Turn right through the farmyard, going first right and then left to pass round the buildings. Behind the last barn a path descends to cross the still-dry riverbed to a gate. Beyond it carry on by an old wall. Before reaching a barn, fork right up an inviting branch path. Here begins the only uphill of the walk, and it will soon reap its rewards. With a few stone steps in place, this zigzags up the steep bank, turning left at the top to meet another grassy zigzag. The upper part runs to a gate to reach Thwaite House. *This former grange of Fountains Abbey is an unexpected oasis of civilisation.*

From a gate to the left of the buildings head off along the access road, a splendid, enclosed cart track that soon emerges into more open country. *You are now treated to spacious views over this great curve of the upper dale, in both directions; the tree-*

lined river winds below, while the dam of Scar House appears under Little Whernside. Reaching Bracken Ridge there is no need to enter the yard. *Note, however, the lovely barn at the top side, with mullioned windows and a 1626 datestone.* Turn up onto the access road heading away to begin a lengthy traverse of The Edge.

Not to be confused with higher level Dale Edge (see WALK 10), this broad track is a splendid platform along which several farms and cottages are based, taking advantage of a spring line in evidence at various locations. Looking ahead, Little Whernside is joined by the shoulder of Great Whernside. With a wall to the left and steep slopes to the right, the track runs pleasurably on to New Houses Edge Farm, last settlement on The Edge. *Only on approaching here does Great Whernside's summit slot into place at the dalehead.* Beyond the farm the track fords a stream to enter an open pasture. Just a little further it forks: take the left branch, descending. This is the turning point as you prepare to return along the dale floor. Reaching a gate near a barn, the track crosses fields to approach the river, which it follows downstream to New Houses Bridge.

Don't cross the shapely structure but go straight ahead to a gate near the river, and along the bank to a stile to continue downstream to avoid New Houses Farm. Follow the Nidd downstream a couple of fields before trading banks at a footbridge. After a pair of neighbouring stiles, Manchester Hole is reached under the cliff of Beggarmoat Scar on the opposite bank. *The Nidd might quietly depart underground here - or it may not. This was the scene of a caving tragedy in 2005 when a member of a school party perished. Note also, up on the road, a bricked-up railway tunnel.*

Only five minutes further, the dark hole of Goyden Pot sits in a crook of the riverbed, reached by tracing the fence downstream, over a slight brow and down to a gate, with the celebrated pothole just beyond. *When the flow of water is sufficiently strong, the excess from Manchester Hole is carried a further 300 yards down to this point. The 'real' Nidd then enjoys a subterranean course for two miles, re-emerging below Lofthouse at Nidd Heads (see WALK 11). While the main chamber can be easily entered, the inner depths contain a maze of passages emphatically only suitable for the well-equipped and experienced caver. If confused by the source of running water in this normally dry environment, turn for an answer to the nearby sidestream of Limley Gill.*

Resume down the grassy bank high above limestone outcrops, crossing Limley Gill and quickly becoming an enclosed grassy way to return to Limley Farm. Enter the yard by a gate to the right of a house, and take the drive out. From here re-trace outward steps through Dry Wath to Thrope Farm, and this time turn down the near side of the buildings on the drive down to the river. Across, take a stile on the left to trace the grassy bank through several stiles. The tree-lined Nidd with its sometimes slabby rock bed is a delight to follow, until forced up onto the road on arrival at a wooded impasse: turn up the bank through a gateway, and on to a gate onto the road at a picnic area.

With its broad verges, the road is dead-level and a pleasure to follow. *This last feature is due to this being the old course of the Nidd Valley Light Railway, constructed by Bradford Corporation in 1908 to transport men and equipment for building the Angram dam at the dalehead. It was dismantled after serving similar work on the Scar House dam, and so this road came into use on the back of the railway's endeavours.* With the road-end in sight ahead, Nidd Falls appear alongside. Stepping over the fence earns a better view of these charming falls in a dark, wooded dell. Then follow a thin path downstream to a stile onto a path alongside a footbridge. Cross the river here, and the path turns to the right up into the centre of Lofthouse.

Limley Farm

NIDD HEAD RESERVOIRS

A level circuit of the two reservoirs that fill the bleak head of Nidderdale: wild surroundings but easy walking

START *Scar House (SE 068766; HG3 5SW)*

DISTANCE *6 miles (9$\frac{1}{2}$km)*

ORDNANCE SURVEY 1:25,000 MAP
Explorer OL30 - Yorkshire Dales North/Central

ACCESS *Just beyond Lofthouse on the Middlesmoor road, a water company road turns off to run the final miles to the dale head car park/WC. • OPEN ACCESS - see page 8.*

From the car park join the water company road which runs past the dam of Scar House Reservoir. This is not crossed until the end of the walk. The road, meanwhile, runs along the entire length of the reservoir's southern shore. *There is a regular supply of benches to rest on, even though you shouldn't exactly need a rest! At the dalehead, the rippling shoulders of Great Whernside form a comprehensive barrier, making it difficult to imagine that such a cosy village as Kettlewell could be only a couple of miles down its other flank. Over to the right is flat-topped Little Whernside.*

The road eventually gains the foot of Angram Reservoir, not seen until you are almost there. Just short of it stands a rest house, a quaint facility provided by the water company, and certainly appreciated if caught by a sudden shower. *Identical in character (though Scar House is double the size) Angram was completed in 1913, 23 years before its lower neighbour. Both the handiwork of Bradford Corporation, each boasts a masonry dam of which Scar House's rises to a height of no less than 150 feet. Beneath Angram's chilly waters is a farm that was once the highest in the dale, on the site of a small grange of Byland Abbey. For the short option cross the dam to pick up the main route at the other end.*

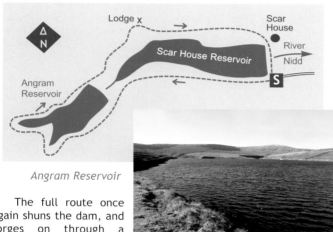

Angram Reservoir

The full route once again shuns the dam, and forges on through a gate/stile to find a good track heading along the shore, indeed crossing the by-wash to put you on the very bank. This later re-crosses the cut, but continues in fine style to very quickly reach the southern arm of the reservoir. Dropping down to the weir on Stone Beck, the track abruptly ends and a path runs on to a footbridge just a little further. Across, double back downstream to a gate, and the path then slants up a bracken bank. The walk's only rougher moments come now as the path forges on across the tussocky tongue of land dividing the two arms of the reservoir. Quickly reaching the northern arm, this proves a longer one as the path briefly ascends to tread the edge of a steeper bank above the waters. Approaching a small ravine, a fence deflects the path down a contrastingly steep little green, dry path to the weir, which this time is crossed directly by way of a long footbridge. *On your left is the infant Nidd, fresh from its birth just a couple of miles westwards high on Great Whernside. This is the furthest point of the walk.*

Across, a broad path slants up to the left, quickly ending above the steeper bank. Turn right on a contrastingly thin trod contouring along the moor. A couple of footbridges cross mere trickles before broadening out to gain the main body of the reservoir again. Now a superb, firm green track takes over, and runs unfailingly on to rapidly return you to the northern end of the dam. Cross straight over onto an equal quality green path, running gently downstream and soon swinging left to begin a contour that is interrupted only by the little dip of Wench Gill. *Enjoy a good view down over the reservoir to Carle Fell and Dale Edge.*

Rising back out to a gate/stile, the path resumes, soon joined by a wall to reach a gate/stile in a fence. Just beyond, a gate/stile admits to the terminus of an enclosed green way. *An option here is to return by the Scar House waterside path, in which case take a stile on the right and descend the wallside to the shore. Go left through a gate/stile to another rest house, then simply trace the excellent path all the way back to the dam.* The main route turns left up the enclosed track which swings right to a junction. Turn right here to almost at once reach the unmistakable cluster of trees around the ruins of the old hamlet of Lodge. *Only scant ruins remain of a medieval hunting lodge that was a working farm until within a century ago. Embowered in trees, this lonely location is prominent in all views around this otherwise bleak dalehead.*

This same track now leads high above Scar House Reservoir's northern shore. *Big views look beyond the dam to the magnificent sweep of the upper valley beneath the moors of Dale Edge. Across the valley, below the car park, is the site of the temporary village that existed during the construction years: here was a complete settlement, with almost 100 children schooled here in the 1920s. On the hillsides, meanwhile, are the sites of quarries opened to win stone for the dams. Everything was on site, including, no doubt, very soon the water!* Another rest house is reached above the dam, with Scar House itself just ahead. Now cross the dam to return to the car park, and take a look back across the dam wall to the extensive Carle Fell Quarry you have just passed beneath.

SLIPSTONE CRAGS

A classic ramble over glorious moorland: massive views over lower Wensleydale and the closer delights of Colsterdale

START *Gollinglith Foot (SE 153809; HG4 4LL)*

DISTANCE *7 miles (11km)*

ORDNANCE SURVEY 1:25,000 MAP
Explorer 302 - Northallerton & Thirsk
Explorer OL30 - Yorkshire Dales North/Central

ACCESS *Start from a parking area by the phone box. Reached from a side road off the Masham-Lofthouse road a good half-mile west of Healey (signed 'Colsterdale'). • OPEN ACCESS - see page 8.*

From the parking area return a few strides along the road and turn up a drive on the left before houses. This runs into a field then climbs steeply towards Agra Crags Plantation. Don't enter but remain on the access road running left towards the farm at Low Agra. Before it, however, turn up outside the plantation wall, ascending a pasture of gorse, rocks and silver birch, with a part sunken old way. *Enjoy views over the farm, with the upper dale driving deep into the moors.* Higher, a clearer track forms, crossing one that links plantations either side, and continuing to a gate in a wall at the top. A fainter grass track continues up the field past rocks to the top corner of the left plantation. Levelling out, it runs on to a gate to become enclosed alongside a higher, smaller plantation at High Agra.

57

Advance along here until just short of the end (not as per map), where take a gate into the field on the left and follow the track around the fieldside to a gate near the far end. An extensive rolling moorland is now spread ahead. The track crosses a field centre, through a fence-gate and temporarily fades as you cross the next pasture to drop left to cross a tiny stream, then rising by an old sunken way to a wall-gate. Again fading, head directly away across the field centre, the high point of this stage. Tranmire farm stands to the left under its belt of trees. Through a gate at the end you enter open access moorland. Though the track heads off right, your grassy path is straight ahead, descending pleasantly through bracken into the heather. *As you drop down, note the Tranmire Stone set into the sturdy wall junction to your left: this boundary stone is inscribed with a hand and 'East Witton' and 'Mashamshire'.*

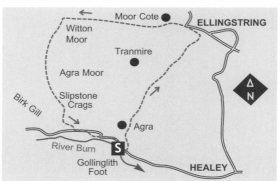

The thin path simply runs along the wallside, over a stream and a small marsh. Passing another boundary stone the way is sent over a ladder-stile (not as per map) to resume on the other side of the wall, through a small gate and on to a plantation corner. Simply forge on the excellent wallside path along this colourful moor. *Further boundary stones are set into the wall.* As you drop towards the end of the moor, fields appear ahead: remain on the moor by dropping left to a green basin surrounded by bracken. Cross to the low brow on its other side, and bear left to pick up an improving track on it. This runs on, slanting towards the road below, but remaining on the moor to meet an access road at the moor corner.

Head left along the rough access road, ignoring its branch to the farm at Moor Cote and remaining on the moor edge to rise to a wall-gate. Through this it forks: the left branch goes to Tranmire, but your way is the right one, striding grandly over Witton Moor alongside a plantation. Levelling out, tracks go out to and return from a shooters' cabin on Tranmire Hill. *Ahead is the profile of Great Roova Crags across the expanse of Caldbergh Moor, and as the plantation ends, things open out to reveal a bigger sweep of your own moor, with Great Haw and South Haw beyond Colsterdale Moor, and the Leyburn area to the right. All this is very, very good.*

Soon after a gentle drop, a crossroads is reached with the East Witton-Colsterdale track coming through a gate on the right. Turn left on the rough way rising gently across the open moor: the watershed crossing onto Agra Moor is marked by a solitary boundary stone to the left and a minor ditch to the right. *At around 1082ft/330m this is the high point of the walk.* Finest feature is the fact that the track at once transforms into a good, firm way, and remains so as it begins a steady decline back into Colsterdale.

As the track becomes stonier Slipstone Crags appear ahead amid glorious mixed scenery as the moor drops away. *Birch-lined Brown Beck tumbles into the woods of Birk Gill at the bottom, with Colsterdale's green pastures on the tongue ahead, and the Burn valley beyond.* Although you can simply remain on this path as it curves down beneath the gritstone edge, better to take a closer look: at a path-side stone before the start of the rocks, a trod turns up to the left, then turns to run along to the crest of the true start. The top of the outcrops can be followed all the way along.

Slipstone Crags is a rock climbers' dream, easy of access and in a beautiful, south-west facing setting. As the rocks fade out, West Agra Plantation is just ahead. A path slants down from the last boulders, through bracken to the wall beside which it descends pleasantly to rejoin the main path as it passes through a gate in the wall. Just yards further take the right branch of this green way, slanting down through bracken to a gate onto the little Colsterdale road. 150 strides left, a thin path slants right through bracken to a gateway stile in the descending wall. Pass right of the garden at Body Close and join the grassy drive at the other side, running out to rejoin the road beneath a hairpin bend. Resume along the road, this final half-mile being a delight in the company of the River Burn.

ILTON MOOR

A bracing stride through the heather above a gorgeous side valley, rounded off by a visit to a remarkable folly

START *Leighton (SE 156787; HG4 4JH)*

DISTANCE *9 miles (14^{1}2km)*

ORDNANCE SURVEY 1:25,000 MAP *Explorer 298 - Nidderdale*

ACCESS *Start from a lay-by just west of the anglers' car park at Leighton Reservoir ('P' on the map denotes the anglers' car park).*

Leighton Reservoir was constructed by Leeds Corporation in the early 20th century, and is a popular fly-fishing venue. Across the waters rise the purple moors that will soon be underfoot. A curiously shaped tower is a sighting tower, one of several erected to aid construction of the aqueduct carrying water to West Riding taps. Heading west along the road, it immediately bridges a finger of the upper reservoir then continues along the shore. As it swings up Pott Bank to Pott Hall Farm en route to Nidderdale, instead bear left over a cattle-grid on a surfaced access road which crosses the fields to Roundhill House. *This is the former reservoir keeper's house dating from 1903.* The continuing road runs along the top of the masonry dam of Roundhill Reservoir. *Pre-dating its neighbour, this one was built by Harrogate Corporation. Both of the dams were supplied with materials by a narrow gauge tramway from the branch line at Masham.*

Immediately across, vacate the main track and opt for the left-hand gate. A track rises up the rough pasture to a track junction in front of a fence. Turn right to a gate in the wall, from where a grassy track ascends to a gate (with an in-built stile) onto Arnagill Moor. Here a distinct, initially grooved track slants up the right, and proves an effortless route onto the tops. *It affords a superb prospect over Roundhill Reservoir to the moorland bounding Upper Nidderdale, and also reveals Leighton Reservoir a long way back.*

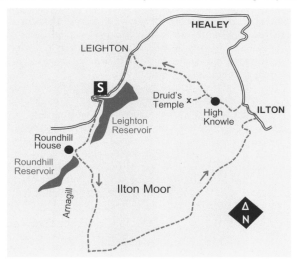

After an initial rise the way runs a largely level course parallel with the side valley of Arnagill down to the right. Characterful boulders are passed, including a huge individual block right by the path. The way reaches the modest outcrops of White Lodge Crags on the right just after crossing a stream. *This splendid vantage point demands an early break.* Resuming, the way runs on to join a broad track. *Visible in advance as it rolls down from the higher moor to the right, this inter-valley route dates from monastic times, connecting Upper Nidderdale with the Masham district. Packhorses would bring lead and wool from the Nidderdale estates for onward carriage to the abbeys at Fountains and Byland.*

Turn left in the foot and hoof steps of history. Over Sandy Hill (at 1168ft/356m the walk's summit on Ilton Moor) the way rolls on. *Extensive views look across to Teesside, Roseberry Topping and the Cleveland and Hambleton Hills.* Gently declining through rampant heather, the track crosses a bridge and promptly forks at the site of High Langwith Cross. While the right branch heads for Kirkby Malzeard, your left fork commences a more pronounced descent. Dropping through heather the moor is finally left at a gate above a plantation. Initially still a track, the way is shortly overlaid by a surfaced farm road. Reaching a junction at the end, forsake the road turning uphill in favour of the colourful walled track down to the left, with a view over to the tall spire of Healey church. On the edge of the scattered hamlet of Ilton its surface returns, passing a former Wesleyan Chapel of 1876.

At the junction by the open green, turn left down the road past the phone box, soon descending sharply to cross Sole Beck. A footbridge waits patiently for a deluge to flood the road. Within 50 yards leave by an enclosed track on the left, soon breaking free to run as a lovely green way outside the plantation. At a gate ignore the stile into the trees and turn up the far side of the wall. A grassy track climbs two fields to High Knowle. *Renovated as 'Bivouac', it offers intriguing accommodation and has a cafe.* Cross a fence-stile at the top and go left outside the buildings and yard, and through a gate join its drive. This rises away through a couple of fields to emerge onto Knowle Lane, the road to the Druid's Temple.

The walk returns to this point after a detour to the folly. Turn left up the road to a car park, and head through Druid's Plantation on a solid track or a green pathway, returning by the other when the temple's environs have been explored. *The Druid's Temple is a folly for which the eccentric British have long been famous. It was constructed in 1820 by William Danby of Swinton Hall, as a useful way of employing his men. Oval in shape, the inner depths lead to 'The Tomb'. The full complement of standing stones is based on the real thing at Stonehenge. Certainly it exudes an atmosphere, particularly if alone on a wild day. Numerous other stone edifices are also spread about the woods.*

Return down the access road and from a stile in the fence on the left, cross the field with a line of telegraph poles bound for a gap in the plantations. *Elaborate gateposts here suggest redundant stones from the temple. Healey and Fearby villages are seen across the valley side beyond. Low Knowle Farm is below in an attractive landscape, with plantations backed by high moorland.* Through the gate go left outside the plantation on a fine, embanked green way to a similar break halfway down. A track comes up from the farm, and once through, turn down the fieldside with the green track that drops down to a ladder-stile. *This superb grassy rake affords extensive views over the Leighton district to Colsterdale's distant moors, while Leighton Reservoir shimmers just ahead.*

From the stile head diagonally left across the field to a stile in a descending fence, in the far corner above a group of trees. *Note the old boundary dyke here.* Continue away, dropping to the edge of a steep wooded bank above Pott Beck. Here a green track forms, slanting right down through scattered woodland, and crossing a track it zigzags down to the beck. Amid delightful surrounds turn upstream to cross a stone-arched bridge. The track climbs a wallside to run right to a gate into a field. Bear right to ascend the fenceside to a farm bridge above a barn, then cross the next field to a gate at the far top corner on the edge of Leighton. Through it turn immediately left (not as per map) to rise up a short green way to the entrance to Leighton Hall Farm, here gaining the road through the farming hamlet. Go left along the Masham-Lofthouse road, concluding alongside Leighton Reservoir.

Roundhill Reservoir from White Lodge Crags

RIVER BURN

Easy rambling in the gentle valley of the Burn, visiting a lovely village before a lengthy spell on delightful riverbanks

START *Masham (SE 225807; HG4 4ED)*

DISTANCE *7 miles (11km)*

ORDNANCE SURVEY 1:25,000 MAP *Explorer 298 - Nidderdale; Explorer 302 - Northallerton & Thirsk*

ACCESS *Start from the town centre. Car parking in the market place. Bus from Ripon, Bedale and Leyburn.*

Masham - pronounced 'Massum' - is a splendid small town above the banks of the Ure. Centrepiece is a massive market square with characterful shops, cottages and the old Town Hall. At one corner stands the church of St Mary the Virgin, its impressive 15th century spire on a Norman base. Attractive 19th century almshouses are spread about, endowed by the Vernon Harcourt family. A modest walking trail links a set of sculptures known as the Masham Leaves. From 1875 Masham had its own station at the terminus of a 7½-mile branch line from Melmerby on the old line north of Ripon, though it closed in 1963. A long-established steam rally is held on the edge of town each July, and a sheep fair in September. Market days are Wednesday and Saturday (charter granted in 1393), while local crafts include glass blowing and pottery. Facilities include a Post office, shops, bank, cafes, a chip-shop and of course pubs.

Masham is a long-established brewing centre, and remarkably in an age of takeovers and closures it has actually doubled its breweries. Theakstons is a Dales institution: in the 1960s a little known yet iconic brewer of then disappearing traditional ales, the real ale revival of the 1970s brought it to the fore. Falling prey to larger brewers it became part of a massive national concern, but happily returned to family independence in 2003. In the former Lightfoot Brewery, neighbouring Black Sheep is aptly named, for a disenchanted member of the Theakston family broke away to start this enterprise in 1992, now a familiar sight on Dales bars. Both breweries have visitor centres and run guided tours.

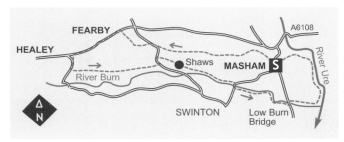

Leave the market place by Church Street, misleadingly at the opposite side to the church. At the bend at Park Square turn briefly right then left along a snicket. At the end this emerges onto Westholme Road alongside Theakston's Brewery. Turn right past the entrance and along the suburban street with a stream. At the sharp bend at the end go left over a stone-arched bridge, and along a lane past a large feeds mill. This ends as the mill does, continuing as a hugely inviting grassy cart track between hedgerows. Opening out into a field continue along the hedgeside, narrowing to a path beyond ramshackle barns to a gate at the end.

Through this turn sharp left over a trickle and along a grassy track to a gate, then bear slightly right across the field to a stile ahead. Bear right around the field, rejoining the grassy fieldside track to a corner gate. Though the track crosses the field centre, your way remains with the hedge on the right to a corner stile, swinging round the corner again and along to emerge onto a back road, Mickleby Lane. *To shorten the walk by a couple of miles*

65

(omitting Fearby), turn down the road for a minute to pick up the return route. Turn right up the tarmac road, briefly, then take a stile on the left. Drop down the hedge as far as a stile in it, with another just yards further in another fence. Now cross to a stile opposite, and on again to one by a plank bridge. Rise to a corner gate just beyond, and a few steps further take a stile on the right. Up above are the houses of Fearby. Simply ascend the hedgeside to a wall-stile at the top, and cross a small enclosure to a gate onto the road through the village.

Turn left and take advantage of the capacious verges. *Fearby is a hugely attractive street village with a pub, the Black Swan, with its own camping/caravan site.* Keep straight on the length of the village, and at the top a footway (which serves the school) is a surprising bonus. *Big views look across the valley to moorland sky-lines beyond.* Before the school, however, take a stile on the left and descend the field to one in another corner below, cutting the corner of a road junction. Descend the road for a couple of minutes just as far as the rough Low Moor Lane on the left. Turn along this for a pleasant, easy stride on an unerring course between hedgerows with good open valley views, eventually arriving back on Mickleby Lane. Turn left up it, briefly, then go right through a gate. A grassy track follows the hedgeside to a gate alongside a small plantation, just past which Shaws Farm appears (as does Masham's church spire).

Bear right towards it, encountering a stile before reaching the farm. Advance into the yard at the rear, but then bear left around the buildings on a fieldside to quickly join a track coming out from the farm. This runs pleasantly above a wooded bank dropping to the River Burn. When the track fades through a gate, bear right to drop down the declining bank to the very riverbank. Just beyond, a gate admits to the edge of Masham golf course. Simply forge straight on the side of the course, keeping faith with the river and ignoring any footbridges. Ultimately the path is deflected away by the clubhouse to cross to a gate onto a road alongside a sturdy stone-arched bridge. A seat tempts you to take a break.

Across the bridge, pass through a stile on the left to resume down the other bank of the river. The golf course remains, though beyond a stile a recommended riverside path keeps you off the course. The riverbank path is grand as you advance downstream, the Burn being good company as it leads to an eroded bend. Around it, the way drops down to cross a colourful pasture to a stile onto the road at Low Burn Bridge. *This is the well-named final bridge on the Burn.*

Cross the bridge and turn right, resuming downstream on a delightful path between hedgerow and wooded bank, amid spring-time carpets of wild garlic. At the end the confluence with the Ure is unseen as a few steps take the path up to join the bank of the principal river. The conclusion is a delectable footpath upstream with the wide-flowing Ure, through lush surrounds. The church spire remains a permanent feature now, to draw you back to the square. This comes beyond a hedgerowed spell at the end, as the path is deflected from the river by the sewage works. An access track takes over to cross the Glebe, past Mill House and back up Millgate into a corner of the market place.

The River Burn at Low Burn Bridge

WEST TANFIELD

The River Ure leads out and back to this charming village,
with two other attractive villages sandwiched in between

START *West Tanfield (SE 269788; HG4 5JY)*

DISTANCE *7 miles (11km)*

ORDNANCE SURVEY 1:25,000 MAP *Explorer 298 - Nidderdale*

ACCESS *Start from the village centre. Car park.*
Bus from Ripon and Masham.

West Tanfield is most favourably viewed from its bridge on
the Ure: dating from around 1734, this fine three-arched structure
makes an impressive gateway into the village. St Nicholas' church
dates back to the 14th century, though much restored in the 19th
century. Among its tombs are splendid effigies of Sir John Marmion
and his wife from around 1400. Alongside the church is the
Marmion Tower, a 600-year old gatehouse to a long-disappeared
manor house: spiral steps lead to the first floor to look over the
village. Alongside the bridge is the Bull Inn, while at the crossroads is the Bruce Arms with its old stables signage. Adjoining the
Methodist Church of 1901 is its predecessor bearing a lintel of
1798. There is also a Post office/shop. This was the only station on
the 7½-mile branch line to Masham, which finally closed in 1963.

Leave by crossing Tanfield Bridge. *Note the perilous stepped*
stile down the right side, though you needn't use it! **The main**

route sets off along a farm road on the right, running to within yards of Quarry House Farm (further than per map) before taking a stile on the left. An enclosed green track runs into a field behind the farm, from where cross diagonally to the river: in the corner is a kissing-gate into the foot of a wooded bank. An alternative start enjoys a permissive riverbank route courtesy of Tanfield Lodge Estate: assuming it is not signed as closed, across the bridge join the river to trace a path upstream around the wide sweep of Greensit Batts, finishing on a flood embankment to enter undergrowth at the rear of Quarry House Farm. The path runs to a stile into the field behind the farm, and beyond that the main route is joined just prior to entering the wood via a kissing-gate near the corner.

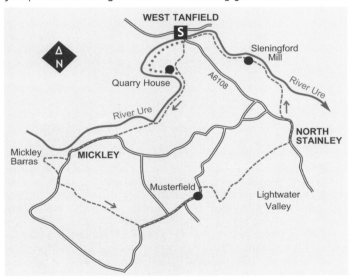

A good path scales the wooded bank then runs on the steep flank before dropping back down. The path runs grandly on to join the river for an excellent stride, and along to a fork on entering trees. To the left is Old Sleningford Farm. Take the left branch along the edge of the wood, over a stone slab on the stream and out into a field. Advance along the wood edge, and at the end a stile leads through a clear break in the wooded belt to emerge, revealing the edge of Mickley ahead. Bear left through park-like surrounds, a line of trees pointing to the nearest cottages, where a stile admits onto a short driveway onto the road at the eastern end of the village. Turn right along the street.

Mickley is a tiny but attractive street village, a riot of spring-time colour. The little church of St John has a bell-cote. At the far end the road climbs away alongside the start of the woodland of Mickley Barras. Part way up, before a steeper climb, a clear path delves into the trees. This runs on to an early fork. Ignore the broader path dropping right, and take that rising slightly left. This continues on closer to the wood top. After dropping to cross a small stream, the path rises to a junction. Here double back left on a thinner but still clear path, which runs a level course beneath the wood top to leave the trees at a gate/stile. Turn left a few steps to another gate/stile beneath a spring, and continue away along the fieldside, following the left-hand hedge all the way to a gate/stile onto a back road.

Turn right a short way, and at the foot of the slope escape left through a gate. A good cart track heads away to a gate into the small copse of Coal Bank Wood. Simply remain on this same bridle-path all the way along, soon emerging to run a delightful course through a part wooded valley alive with bluebells. Ultimately the path swings right at the end to a gate out of the trees. Advance along the hedgeside (beware of a moist moment) and on to a gate at the end, then swinging around to a gate onto a back road at Frizer Hill. Go left, enjoying a superb springtime daffodil display for half a mile, and ignoring junctions to left and right. *At the Ripon one, note an old boundary stone inscribed 'Musterfield 1837'.*

Passing Musterfield Farm, the path diverts to avoid a quarry. Advance to the bend after the farm, and a few strides further take a gateway in the hedge on the right. The bridleway doubles back right along the fieldside and down the wood edge to join a firm track at the bottom. Turn right on this, soon encountering the deep, working quarry on your right. Part way along the track swings sharp left, passing further old quarries alongside Fiveponds Wood before running more pleasantly on, and slowly down, with views to the North York Moors. The improving way drops steadily down until a sharp turn right. With North Stainley in view just ahead, pass through a gate in front to maintain the straight line, down a field-side to a kissing-gate at the end. Pass through the suburbia of Cock Pit Close onto the A6108 through North Stainley.

Cross the road and turn left along the verge. *North Stainley is a straggling main road village with attractive ponds on open greens, and the Staveley Arms pub. Just opposite the cricket pitch is the modest mid-19th century church of St Mary the Virgin with its bell-cote. Unseen on the southern edge of the village is the vast and popular theme park of Lightwater Valley.* Keep straight on out of the village and leave by the penultimate drive on the right just before the de-restriction sign. Follow the drive to the end cottage, where the path slips down to the right between gardens. Ignoring a small gate ahead, the path goes to its left to run an enclosed course between a pond on the left and a large field on the right.

Further along the base of this scrubby bank, the path ascends a few wooden steps to the top, and takes a bridle-gate just to your right. Now on the bank top, within a few strides take a bridle-gate in the adjacent fence and resume along the fieldside for a few strides to suddenly arrive at a splendid vantage point overlooking a fine curve of the Ure. The path then simply traces the bank top upstream past a recently eroded section. Soon the path runs into trees and along to a better grassy way, with the river now hidden beyond the scrub of Mill Batts.

Entering a caravan site the path runs to the reception buildings, including a small shop. To the right is the splendidly-sited Sleningford Watermill, with the wide-flowing river popular with canoeists. Follow the access road out, and a little beyond the gates, where it turns up towards the main road, take a path to the right to remain with the river. This traces the Ure upstream past a wide weir on a bend to return to the bridge at West Tanfield.

Pond, North Stainley

An extended ramble through beautiful woodland above the Ure

START *Grewelthorpe (SE 231761; HG4 3BS)*

DISTANCE *6^{1}2 miles (10^{1}2km)*

ORDNANCE SURVEY 1:25,000 MAP *Explorer 298 - Nidderdale*

ACCESS *Start from the village centre. Roadside parking.*
Very infrequent Ripon-Masham bus.

Grewelthorpe is a linear village featuring attractive cottages set back from spacious greens. St James' church has a small bell turret, while a Methodist chapel stands redundant. A sloping green at the west end overlooks the Crown Inn, while towards the other end is a colourful pond. Leave the village by its eastern end, and a short way beyond the pond, as the road narrows to leave, take a gate on the left from where a splendid hedgerowed cart track heads away into rolling country. This soon drops down to swing right to a field, but take the gate in front and an even better green way runs a gem of an enclosed course. At the end ignore the gate in front, and take a stile on the right to resume along the holly hedgeside. From a stile at the end cross to a stile in the facing hedge, then bear left to one in the fence.

Head away to a stile opposite, and on again to the far end of the field, with a gate revealing Bush Farm in front. Cross to a stile in the hedge ahead, then bear right to the far corner of the field, keeping left of all farm buildings to drop to a gate in the corner. Entering a rougher slope, keep right with the fence as far as an old gateway, then drop down through a gate into the field below. Descend to the field bottom, then go left with the hedge outside the wood to a gate/stile in the corner, by a spring. Yards further take a gate/stile on the right into the woodland of Mickley Barrass.

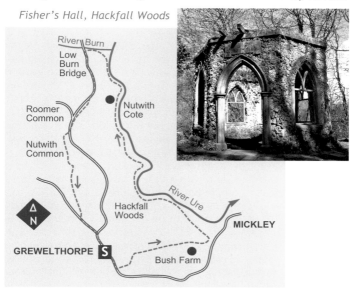

Fisher's Hall, Hackfall Woods

A good path heads away, running a level course to meet a broader path. Turn left to soon enjoy a splendid stride through the trees. Ignore a thinner branch rising left, and forge on through a bracken clearing, passing above a circular pool. Dropping down, cross a tiny stream to enter Hackfall Woods. *Acquired by the Woodland Trust in the 1980s, these were landscaped and filled with an assortment of 18th century follies and grottoes by William Aislabie of Studley Royal, and have only recently been restored: Victorian visitors paid to explore this fascinating setting.* There now follows a sustained mercurial section closer to the river, with steep banks above, and seasonal wild garlic carpets all around. After a stream crossing, with an island in the river alongside, three ways depart. Take the central one, with inviting old stone steps climbing to Fisher's Hall, a folly unexpectedly lurking just above. *A stone lintel carved 'WA 1730' is a reminder of Aislabie.*

Take the broad path continuing along a neck of land, at once joined by the earlier left branch. A little further is a fork, remain on the main, right branch. This leads to a staggered crossroads, with a branch doubling back left. Instead cross the stream in front, and another fork. *The left branch offers a two-minute detour as a super path rises to another folly, this of rougher hewn blocks alongside a pond.* Back at the fork the lower path runs grandly on, dropping through rampant wild garlic and absorbing the earlier lower path and around a big river bend. Just beyond, the public path is signed uncertainly left, as a much thinner path rising up the bank away from the broad riverside way: they soon re-unite. The upper path does a neat little zigzag featuring old stone steps, to quickly surmount the brow of Limehouse Hill. *This reveals a fine cameo ahead of the river backed by Masham's tall church spire.*

A little further the broader path rejoins, and you run on to a corner of the wood. While a path rises left, take the kissing-gate in front and head along a field bottom outside the trees. Further on, a kissing-gate re-admits to Nutwith Cote Wood, and a good path slants down through plantations to the riverbank. This now runs a super course upstream, rising at the end on a track to a gate out of the trees. Ignore the green track continuing up, and return to the steep wooded bank above the river, tracing this to drop just before the end to a stile below. Up above is Nutwith Cote Farm. Even more enjoyable walking takes over as you trace the grassy bank upstream. Further, the inflowing River Burn deflects the path away from the Ure. Tracing the soon to be revealed beck, a grassy way runs upstream to the road at Low Burn Bridge. *This is the well-named final bridge on the Burn (see page 67).*

Double back left along the road for a good half-mile to enter the open country of Roomer Common. At once bear left on a cart track rising away, running a super course up the common. *Looking back, Masham is dominated by its tall spire.* Higher, as you near the road, keep on a narrower way between wall and scrub, running a parallel course to the road to only rejoin it at the very end of the common. Here cross to the foot of the plantations of Nutwith Common. Follow the hard track just a few strides then bear left on a clear, more inviting footpath. This rises grandly through the trees to meet a forest road. Cross straight over to the left-hand path ascending stiffly to join a higher forest track. The continuation is unclear: go right fifty paces and a faint path rises left to quickly join an excellent path on the wood-top ridge. Go left on this a short way until a clear path branches right, dropping to a gate in a wall out of the trees. A slender trod slants left up the scrubby bank to a stile. *Pause here to look east over the vale to the Hambleton Hills fronting the North York Moors, with Whitestone Cliff prominent.*

Through the stile rise a short way with the hedge then take a stile in it. *Over to the left is an Ordnance Survey column at 705ft/215m on Horsepasture Hill, but more interesting is the well-defined bank of an ancient enclosure, highlighted by an old wall. Big views look south towards Kirkby Malzeard with the Dallowgill moors beyond, and the edge of Grewelthorpe in view just below.* A path slants diagonally down to a stile opposite. Continue the slant down the next field to another stile. The final field is crossed to the opposite corner, though if ploughed it is easier to keep left along the wallside, following the grassy headland past Hedgehog House and around to a stile onto a road. Go left along its verges to the edge of the village, bearing right at the sloping, triangular green by the old smithy to re-enter the main street.

The River Ure at Hackfall Woods

LAVER COUNTRY

A leisurely amble round villages above the River Laver, free of crowds, entirely rural, visiting many places of interest

START Kirkby Malzeard (SE 235743; HG4 3RY)

DISTANCE 8 miles (13km)

ORDNANCE SURVEY 1:25,000 MAP Explorer 298 - Nidderdale

ACCESS Start from the village centre: the walk begins from the eastern end. Roadside parking. Occasional Ripon-Masham bus.

Kirkby Malzeard is a lengthy street village, and the one-time administrative centre of a vast area. A market charter was granted in 1307, and a replacement buttercross of 1868 occupies the main crossroads. A circular pinfold stands at one end of the village. Markets and fairs drew the monks of Fountains and Byland, who came by way of moorland roads from their Nidderdale estates. On a wooded knoll behind the village stood the castle of Roger de Mowbray, son of Nigel de Albini who came over with the Conqueror. A 500-year old tower and a Norman doorway remain at St Andrew's church, much rebuilt after 1908 fire damage: the mouse symbol of Robert Thompson of Kilburn is in evidence in the Lady Chapel. The church is surrounded by some very old gravestones. A unique pub name celebrates the longevity of Henry Jenkins, born in 1500 and who supposedly lived an astonishing 169 years. There is a second pub, the Queens Head, also a shop, tearoom and chip-shop.

Leave the cross by turning east along the Ripon road. *Set back on the left is the rather grand Mowbray House, beyond which is Wensleydale Creamery's Kirkby Malzeard dairy.* The road descends to Creets Bridge. *Note the proud gateposts on the left, with coats of arms, alongside attractive woodland.* Over the bridge, turn right along the drive towards Lawnwith Farm with the stream alongside. Leave however, at a kissing-gate on the left before entering the trees. From a stile at the end cross a field to a stile opposite, then rise away with a fence. Beyond an intervening stile keep on past the edge of a wood. From its corner a thin path crosses the centre of a crop field.

The maypole, Galphay

At the end sanity returns in the appealing sheep pastures of Azerley Park. Head directly away, and beyond an intervening stile a fence is followed towards the trees at Azerley. At the end bear right to a stile by a gate, entering a lawn with a house just ahead. Fork immediately right on a super green pathway through the woods in the company of Kex Beck. Ignore an early fork left and remain with the beck. Passing a pond it runs on through trees and past a cottage to the access road into Azerley: cross straight over and along the drive past Grange Farm to Home Farm. The track

77

continues past it and runs on for a considerable time, often between hedgerows. Ignoring left turns to the folly of Azerley Tower and then Eight Acre Wood, the track swings right and drops appreciably. It ends at the bottom as two hedgerows head away. A waymark confirms you turn left alongside a sparse hedge towards the wood at the end. Swing right outside the trees and drop to a stile just below, then cross to a footbridge on Kex Beck.

In the field behind, cross to a clump of trees secreting the Witch-of-the-Woods House. *Though first impression is of a ruinous barn, a glimpse through the surround of trees sees a mysterious residence: on my 1993 visit stiles gave access, and a glance inside revealed a simply furnished room, complete with a table set for a meal. Since seeing renovation, today its privacy is underlined by a gate marked private.* On the other side rise right to a gate in the fence opposite. Through it a grassy track runs left along the other side, through more gates and along to Cow Myers Farm. Head between the buildings and out along its drive onto the Galphay-Ripon road above the River Laver.

Cross straight over and along the drive to Galphay Wood. The drive runs on through lovely park-like grounds high above the river. When the house appears just ahead, leave by a gate on the right and follow the opposite side of the hedge along past the house, to a corner gate. The edge of an unkempt enclosure leads to a second gate into a better field. Horse-riders are requested to stay on the (invisible) track, an informal diversion from the right of way. This runs left, through a gate and up the fieldside to another gate just short of Laver Banks Farm. The right of way ascends the hedgeside on your right, to step over a fence in a gap in the hedge at the top. Here turn left to a contrastingly splendid stile in a hedge, then rise right alongside the hedge. At the top corner pass through a small wooded bank at the top corner and along above the farm to join its drive at the end. Ahead is the bulky tower of Winksley church, and the drive leads down into the village.

Tiny Winksley overlooks the Laver and is dominated by the church of St Cuthbert & St Oswald, just along to the left. It dates from 1917, on the site of a chapel built by Abbot Marmaduke Huby of Fountains Abbey. For a tiny circuit, take the road down the near side of the churchyard to a crossroads, then turn right past the phone box and attractive cottages. *Countryman House on the right is the former Countryman Inn, a fairly recent casualty of modern times, when rural pubs far often offer greater value as residential property.* Rejoining the top road turn left to leave the village along the lane above Winksley Banks.

While the easy option is to remain on the road to a junction where turn right for Galphay, a short-cut path takes a gate on the right just before the road swings left into trees. Bear left to a small gate in the field corner, and maintain this line down to another such gate part way along the field edge (paralleled by a fence you must use as a hurdle stile). From this descend the adjacent hedge-side along to a gate onto West Lane just left of a barn (not quite as per map, which shows a way out of the field corner). Go right into Galphay.

Galphay boasts a hugely attractive village centre with its many clusters of colourful cottages and gardens. Its large, sloping green sports a tall maypole restored in 1999, while a small stream tinkles through a smaller, lower green. A circular pinfold on your approach to the village was restored in 2002 by the Lord of the Manor, and its delightful garden makes the perfect spot for a refreshment break - as does the Galphay Inn, of course!

Turn left at the green past the Galphay Inn to a sharp bend, where impressive gates front a drive which would lead directly to Braithwaite Hall. A more attractive alternative route goes briefly left on the road, taking a kissing-gate on the right at a junction. An invisible path runs on through the park grounds, parallel with the drive. Beyond a miry pond it swings right to join the drive at a cattle-grid to enter the inner grounds, with farm buildings to the left. Take the main drive ahead, curving left down to the front of the hall. *Architecturally very characterful, its great roof appears to entirely overburden the stone walls beneath. On the right is a large duckpond.*

Immediately in front of the hall turn sharp right, as the drive heading away transforms into a green way. At the end take the right-hand gate to enter a large sheep pasture. Keep near to the left-hand fence to descend to a corner gate. Through it, an access track is joined to lead back over Kex Beck to Lawnwith and its drive onto the road at Creets Bridge. Return up the road, noting, immediately after the dairy, a dark snicket offering a conclusion by way of the churchyard.

FOUNTAINS ABBEY

Unparalleled beauty in this sumptuous promenade around a designated World Heritage Site

START *Fountains Abbey (SE 272686; HG4 3DY)*

DISTANCE *5 miles (8km)*

ORDNANCE SURVEY 1:25,000 MAP *Explorer 298 - Nidderdale or Explorer 299 - Ripon & Boroughbridge*

ACCESS *Start from the National Trust Visitor Centre off the B6265 Pateley Bridge-Ripon road, almost 3 miles west of Ripon. Buses from Ripon. There is an appreciable (though worth every penny) entry fee to the Abbey for non-National Trust members. Open daily from 10am, except Christmas Eve, Christmas Day, and Fridays in January, November and December.*

   Leaving the visitor centre the surfaced path immediately forks: take the right branch, curving through trees then out into an open pasture - revealing a first view of the abbey tower - to a gate into a wooded bank. Take the left branch down to the abbey. *Set forth to explore the delights of this staggeringly beautiful ruin, the most extensive Cistercian remains in England. Fountains Abbey was founded in 1132 by a group of dissatisfied Benedictine monks from St Mary's Abbey in York: seeking a stricter routine they turned to the French Cistercian order. Though it would have been a much wilder place then, the setting they chose could be matched only by perhaps Bolton and Rievaulx. Built largely between the mid 12th and 13th centuries, this was one of the most important religious houses. Whilst their granges occupied much of nearby Nidderdale, their possessions stretched to the Cumberland fells. Dairy farming, lead mining and other industry also came within their scope: many ordinary peoples' lives revolved around the abbey. Perhaps the abbey's finest feature is the 300ft long west range, the remarkable vaulted cellarium. Most impressive is the 180ft high tower, a 16th century addition built by Abbot Marmaduke Huby: it remained incomplete at the Dissolution.*

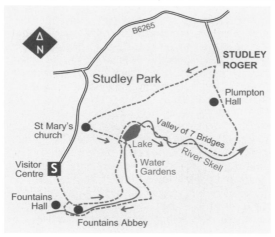

Rejoining the main carriageway, scars on the left show evidence of quarrying for the great building programme. Surfaced through-out, the drive provides a smashing walk along to the water gardens, regarded, once again, as the finest in the country. *Since the Trust's acquisition of the estate in the early 1980s, these superb gardens have been comprehensively restored to once again resemble the beautiful scene created throughout the 1700s by the new owners, the Aislabie family. All the buildings such as the temples and the Octagon Tower were added during this period.*

Beyond a bend above Half Moon Pond, running above the canalised Skell you are treated to views over the Moon Pond, flanked by crescents and with lead statues in attendance, to the Temple of Piety: high above, meanwhile, are other features for the return journey. At the eastern end of the grounds another shop sees you out past a ticket office to emerge at the lake and the Studley Royal deer park. *Here also is a tearoom and WC.*

Follow the drive alongside the lake, and at the end remain with the lake on a track to the outflow. Here begins the walk through the Valley of Seven Bridges, the first being a wooden one over the outflow. *Look back from here to see the spire of St Mary's church silhouetted high above the deer park.* The River Skell is accompanied downstream through this steep-sided valley, a delightful amble that re-crosses the river on five further occasions by means of identical stone arched bridges. After the last one the estate is vacated, temporarily, at a tall kissing-gate, and a wood-land path runs down to pass the seventh bridge (this plain structure is not crossed) before the track climbs the wooded bank to leave the river. Out of the trees it runs a pleasant fieldside course with open views. *Most remarkable aspect is the immediate appearance of Ripon Cathedral little more than a stone's throw away, with a long line of the Hambleton Hills beyond.*

Passing mellow-walled Plumpton Hall and its farm buildings, the track becomes surfaced to reach the edge of Studley Roger at a lodge and a small green. *This little village features attractive cottages with red pantile roofs. Look right along the carriageway which forms a perfect alignment with the cathedral and the church.* Go left on the estate drive, through the East Entrance arch to re-enter the park. Strolling along the broad driveway, St Mary's church is framed beyond the long avenue of limes. *In the heart of the centuries-old deer park many of these creatures can be seen, with Red, Fallow (most numerous) and Sika deer all present.* When cars are sent left to the car park above the lake, either go with them, or incorporate a visit to the church by remaining on the drive. *St Mary's was built in 1871-78, boasting an impressive great spire prominent in many views around the neighbourhood. It is open on afternoons from Easter to October. A tall obelisk of 1815 stands just behind the church.* From the church a grassy path descends to the east entrance to the abbey by the lake.

Re-entering, turn left and cross the Skell as it enters the lake, either by footbridge or stepping-stones. The path heads back past the water gardens, but just before reaching the Temple of Piety, a high-level alternative offers itself. Doubling back up, pass through the dark-walled Serpentine Tunnel to emerge by the Octagon Tower. *This provides good views over the smaller Half Moon Pond and much of the grounds, including the Banqueting Hall opposite, and the church spire.* Continuing, the broad path runs on past the Temple of Fame to Surprise View at Ann Boleyn's Seat. *The surprise at this wooden shelter is the sudden return of the abbey to the scene, in dramatic style beyond a sharp bend of the river.* Just past here the path doubles back down the wooded bank to rejoin the lower one at Half Moon Pond. Turning left the way runs on by the river to return to the abbey, passing Robin Hood's Well en route. One can turn down to the start of the ruins for further exploration, or remain on the path above the abbey to arrive at the old abbey mill. Here the path returns to join the main carriageway.

Along to the left is Fountains Hall. With its intricate facade this magnificent house was completed in 1611, much of the stone being plundered from the abbey that had only been abandoned in 1539. Last private owners were the Vyner family, descendants of the Aislabies, and evidence of their presence includes a particularly touching memorial in the hall entrance stairway. Return to the starting point by following the surfaced path up the wooded bank.

Fountains Hall

EAVESTONE LAKE

Charming rolling estate country leads by a string of historic features to the lovely wooded lakes of Eavestone

START Sawley (SE 248677; HG4 3EE)

DISTANCE 5 miles (8km)

ORDNANCE SURVEY 1:25,000 MAP Explorer 298 - Nidderdale

ACCESS Start from the expansive green-cum-playing fields. Ample car parking alongside. Occasional bus from Ripon.

Sawley is a small but outwardly affluent village in the estate country west of Fountains Abbey. The tiny church of St Michael & All Angels is on the site of a chapel built by Abbot Marmaduke Huby of Fountains. A bell remains in place on a former schoolhouse at the top of the green, while the village pub is the Sawley Arms. From the green walk back through the village between church and pub to a T-junction. From a stile in the facing wall head away across the field, bearing gently away from the road over to your left. From a gate/stile at the other side, head away with a hedge on the left, at the far end joining a driveway through the fields.

Bear right on this to a cattle-grid at the entrance to Lacon Hall. *Mullioned windows form part of an attractive frontage dating from the 16th century.* Don't enter but turn right on the fieldside to the corner. Bear left to another corner, slanting gently away from the grounds, through a line of scrub, and on to a wall ahead.

Turn up its near side to a plantation at the top. *This faint path shows signs of causeying, being distinctly raised in parts.* From a stile at the top corner cross diagonally to a similar corner, passing close by Lacon Cross. *Astride a route west from Fountains Abbey to Nidderdale, this wayside cross on its solid base has a hollowed top.* At the corner a stile admits onto well-named Green Lane. Go right to emerge into a vast field amid a thorough surround of dark plantations. Aim across the field, bearing right of the one visible farm amid green fields opposite. Locate a small gate admitting to the plantation in front, alongside an elaborate spring.

A broad track slants down to the right, but leave almost at once by a path dropping left off it. This descends a steep wooded bank onto a forest road, crossing straight over to cross the ancient Butterton Bridge on Picking Gill. *Its stone arch is yet more evidence of this centuries-old route.*

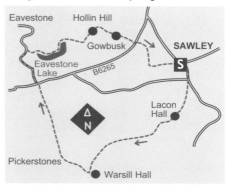

A grassy cart track continues away from the beck above a smaller side beck. As it swings steeply left uphill, advance straight on a path, keeping company with the sidestream. This splendid sunken way rises below a collapsed wall before reaching another gate out of the woods. Rise to a gateway above, then head up the fieldside to a gate at the top corner. From it head away to locate a wall-stile to the right of farm buildings of Warsill Hall.

Turn right on a wallside track towards impending plantations. Through a gate near a plantation corner on the left, the track crosses a field centre to the next gate, with the realisation that the great swathes of plantation must surely envelop you before long! Another wallside leads on to the right-hand of two gates, into a plantation corner. The map falsely suggests this last field on the left is also a plantation. The grand enclosed way runs inside the plantation boundary to join the bend of a forest road. Advance directly along this, running straight as a die through the heart of the High Moor plantation. Ignoring any branches - including the main track's swing left - it rises gently to leave the plantation at a gate. A green track runs on outside the boundary wall, soon leaving the trees completely. *Big views return, with Kirkby Malzeard Moor on the left skyline.* Dropping to a gate onto the B6265 Pateley Bridge-Ripon road, cross straight over and down the Eavestone cul-de-sac.

Down past the farm, as the road swings sharply left, descend a little then take a path doubling back into the wood. Here begins a glorious spell on a brilliant path in magnificent surroundings. First feature is the upper reservoir above Eavestone Lake, with a dark crag jutting into the water. *The gritstone surrounding these two lakes is a goldmine for climbers, yielding climbs of all standards on at least sixteen separate buttresses: some literally overhang your path by the main lake.* Crossing its outflow the path winds round to the head of Eavestone Lake, along which it runs the full length. *Of immediate interest are the forbidding outcrops of Ravens Crag towering above the opposite bank. Abundant water-fowl, spring bluebells and wild garlic amid the luxuriant foliage of this mixed woodland combine to provide a half-hour of delight.*

At the end fork right to cross a small dam and a little arched bridge: penance awaits in the form of a sustained pull through Fishpond Wood. A gate at the top consigns the Eavestone scene to memory, as you pass round the left side of a field to join the drive to Hollin Hill Farm. Take its drive round to the back, and go straight on through a gate into a scrubby corner. Advance into the field corner and keep right to quickly find a ladder-stile into a slim enclosure. As it opens out keep with its right side to run to West Gowbusk. Go straight through the farmyard and out along the drive, but quickly leave by a private-looking gate on the left. This accesses the front of a cottage at Gowbusk, to follow its drive out to the B6265. Go briefly left and take a stile on the right: Sawley appears ahead.

Cross the field to a far corner stile, then rise gently along the fieldsides. *Note the prominent spire of Studley Royal church and perhaps a glimpse of Fountains Abbey's tower in the intervening rolling country.* Entering a rough enclosed lane, leave at once by a stile on the left and descend the fieldside. A stile at the bottom admits to a short-lived hedgerowed path. A stile at the end sends you down fieldsides to re-enter the village green via a wall-stile.

RIPON'S RIVERS

Very leisurely walking on Ripon's leafy riverbanks

START Ripon (SE 312712; HG4 1BX)

DISTANCE 5$\frac{1}{4}$ miles (8$\frac{1}{2}$km)

ORDNANCE SURVEY 1:25,000 MAP
Explorer 299 - Ripon & Boroughbridge

ACCESS Start from the Market Square. Car parks.
Bus from Leeds, Harrogate, Boroughbridge and York.

The smallest of Yorkshire's cities is an outstanding market 'town' dominated by a beautiful Cathedral on the 7th century site of Wilfrid's monastery. Though the present building dates from the 12th century, the Saxon crypt of 672 still survives. The West front presents a stunning high wall filling the end of Kirkgate, and internal delights include the east window and a medieval screen. The Market Square is Ripon's buzzing heart, and Thursday markets present an animated scene, centrepiece being a tall obelisk of 1702. For many centuries Ripon was under ecclesiastical rule known as The Liberty, with the Archbishop of York's authority being greater than that of the King. Under this arrangement a 'Wakeman' was responsible for townsfolk's safety during the hours of darkness, and this setting of the watch was heralded by the sounding of a horn in the Market Cross, a millennium-old tradition maintained at 9pm each evening.

Overlooking the square is the Town Hall of 1801, while just doors away is the Wakeman's House with its Tudor facade. Many central street names are still 'gates', a layout little changed since medieval times. Ripon's greatest change came as recently as 1996, when waggons bound for the A1 were finally diverted from congested streets onto a by-pass. Other buildings of interest include Cathedral Hall on the site of a medieval school, with the red-brick Old Hall of 1738 in adjacent Minster Close. Other attractions are the tiny Ripon Canal linked to the Ure, and only brought back to life in the 1990s. Ripon had a brief flirtation with the spa boom thanks largely to mineral springs discovered at nearby Aldfield. Ripon also boasts one of Yorkshire's many famous racecourses, while the Law & Order Museums occupy the rather gaunt Victorian surroundings of the Courthouse, Workhouse and House of Correction.

From the market place head on Kirkgate to the awesome west front of the cathedral. Bear right along its outer wall, and part way along turn down a firm path, under an arch and out past Cathedral Hall onto High St Agnesgate: turn right. *On your left is a Norman arch of the*

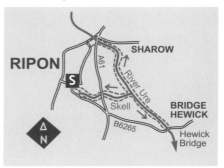

chapel of St Anne's Hospital, an early almshouse, while Thorp Prebend House is a medieval Canon's house open to visitors as a heritage centre. At the end turn left just as far as Bondgate Bridge on the River Skell. *From here the river makes a fine foreground to the imposing cathedral.* Across, take steps down to the bank and follow an urban path downstream. This passes a footbridge by the Water Rat pub and onto a road at a ford and footbridge. Continue downstream, now on the road at Fishergreen and soon passing beneath the by-pass for the first time. *The stone arches survive from Ripon's former railway, cynically utilised by modern road builders.* At the end a path takes over, delving into trees to remain true to the Skell to its demise at the confluence with the Ure.

The path turns downstream with the major river, still cloaked in greenery, and though forced up onto a grassy flood embankment part way along, this course remains outside the scrubby bank to reach Hewick Bridge. Cross and resume up the east bank. *The Blackamoor pub at Bridge Hewick is just minutes further on the road. Note also, as you get going, the concrete remains of a ford utilized by tanks during Second World War training manouevres.* The path retains its course upstream, sometimes through scrub, often on the true wooded bank, and generally very nicely all the way to emerge at the Sharow road, without joining it. Instead the path shadows the river under the by-pass and along to the edge of North Bridge, Ripon's major river crossing. Cross and turn left on Magdalen's Road.

Very quickly, at a bend, pass through an old iron kissing-gate and a path heads off back to the river, again shadowing it under the by-pass and resuming downstream in delightful surrounds to rejoin the Skell. The path turns back upstream with Ripon's own river, and though briefly away from it, it runs to a kissing-gate by a house, onto its short drive and back under the by-pass. A suburban street runs on, but at the first chance turn left to meet the Skell again at the earlier ford/footbridge. Turn up the near side on a path back to the Water Rat. Either cross the bridge to finish as you began, or turn right on the short street to return to the cathedral yard.

Cathedral from the Skell

RIPON CANAL

The gentle banks of the River Ure lead to a delightful encounter with the towpath of a restored waterway

START Bishop Monkton (SE 329662; HG3 3QU)

DISTANCE 6 miles (9½km)

ORDNANCE SURVEY 1:25,000 MAP
Explorer 299 - Ripon & Boroughbridge

ACCESS Start from the village centre. Roadside parking.
Bus from Ripon, Knaresborough and Harrogate.

Bishop Monkton is a lovely village whose quality features are enhanced by a stream through the centre. The church of St John the Baptist boasts a tall spire, and there are two pubs. Head south from the Lamb & Flag along the main street in company with the stream. At the end turn left opposite the Masons Arms, along an enclosed rough lane, Ings Lane. *A modest brow affords a brief glimpse of the White Horse of Kilburn on the Hambleton Hills beyond the Vale of York.* Remain on its dead straight course all the way past a house and on to a fork: as the main way turns sharp right, keep straight on down a softer track to the bottom just below, where it fades. A leafy enclosed footway takes over, swinging left and then running a grand course before emerging into a field. Keep straight on over a stile ahead and along the hedgeside, which terminates just short of a gate onto Boroughbridge Road.

Turn briefly left, and at the village/30mph sign, take a small gate on the right. Head away through a gate and remain on the fieldside, at the corner a firm path takes over and continues along a minor embankment by a stream. This winds along to emerge into another field. *There are glimpses of the red-brick Newby Hall ahead across the currently unseen river.* At the end the bank of the Ure is gained. Turn left to commence a delightful stretch upstream with the wide-flowing river. Initially on an embankment, this soon turns off leaving you to trace the lush bank upstream, soon reaching a major deflection caused by the Ripon Canal. At this pleasant spot the river widely departs, while your path runs to Oxclose Lock just ahead.

The lock was built in order to convey boats from the Ure onto the two mile long Ripon Canal. This was the northernmost limit of the Ure Navigation, constructed in 1772 to enable riverborne freight to access the city. Coal was the principal import into Ripon, while lead mined in nearby Nidderdale found its way out of the Dales from here. This little waterway was abandoned during the mid 20th century after long since losing trade to the railway, but restoration in the 1990s has seen it become a fine addition to Ripon's attractions, and a much valued local leisure facility. During the course of World War Two the lock saw military use, for training divers.

A grassy track now heads along the waterside, soon joined by a surfaced access road along to the arch of Rentons Bridge. Cross the bridge and resume on a grassy path along the other bank. *Just over the hedge is Ripon racecourse, while on the other side is Ripon Motor Boat Club.* Next bridge is Nicholsons Bridge, where you leave the canal. Cross it and follow a muddy lane along to a road bend in Littlethorpe. Turn left to a junction by St Michael's church of 1878. Go left on Pottery Lane, passing through the scattered community and a couple of sharp bends, then out past further scattered houses. Beyond them all the road turns sharp right, and here leave it by advancing straight on the left-hand drive in front at Fairfield. To the right is a fishery.

Past a couple of contrasting houses this firm track passes left of a couple of long poultry sheds and away along the fieldside. At a junction at the end go just a few strides left and escape by a stile on the right. Head away along the hedgeside, with Bishop Monkton appearing ahead. A firm track comes in to join you, advance along it swinging left and then leaving the fence to run to a tiny stream crossing. As it fades just beyond, keep straight on a faint grassy way to a gate/stile ahead. From a stile just beyond, an enclosed path leads back along a fieldside to emerge onto a short drive to re-enter the village. Go right to finish, past the Mechanics Institution of 1859 and possibly bearing left to conclude alongside the duck-dabbling stream by the neat old Main Street.

A corner of Bishop Monkton

COPGROVE

Three unassuming villages linked by charming rural ways

START *Burton Leonard (SE 327638; HG3 3SJ)*

DISTANCE *6^{1}2 miles (10^{1}2km)*

ORDNANCE SURVEY 1:25,000 MAP
Explorer 299 - Ripon & Boroughbridge

ACCESS *Start from the village centre. Roadside parking.
Bus from Ripon, Knaresborough and Harrogate.*

Burton Leonard is a colourful village grouped around an arrangement of greens. St Leonard's church of 1878 stands to one corner, along with a red-brick Methodist church, a village school, the Royal Oak pub, a Post office/shop and the old village pump in a shelter on the lower green. Head east from the centre, past the church and a second pub, the Hare & Hounds, leaving the village on Mill Lane. *From the brow views look east to the Hambleton Hills: visible is the White Horse of Kilburn, along with a much closer and equally celebrated Yorkshire landmark, Ripon Cathedral.*

At a crossroads go straight across and down with a verge, until a turning branches right. Take this, and remain on this access lane to a cattle-grid at the end of a wood. At this path crossroads the access road bears right towards Crow House: your route is straight ahead on a lesser track. Beyond a stile/gate in a fence this improves into a good track, running on past another wood edge to approach a big modern barnyard. While the track swings right to ford Holbeck, you have the option of a footbridge straight ahead.

Now turn right to a gate/stile onto the access road, and go right along it, briefly, passing a pond. Level with Well House, ignore its drive rising away and instead take a gate on the right. Head away outside the wood, holding to the fence on your left to rise pleasantly to a cluster of houses at Copgrove. Advance through a stile and on to a snicket behind, running between hidden gardens to emerge onto an access road, St Mongah's Lane. Go straight ahead on this suburban driveway to emerge at a junction with the through road, alongside a church. *The little church of St Michael & All Angels has a bell-cote and Norman origins.* Turn right on the verge, leaving the village and ignoring a branch left at a lodge. The verge leads all the way to your turning, where a surfaced way slants left after a directly ascending drive. This comes just before the road drops to bridge a lake. *It is worth continuing to this point to appraise the large lake, a fine foreground to Copgrove Hall.*

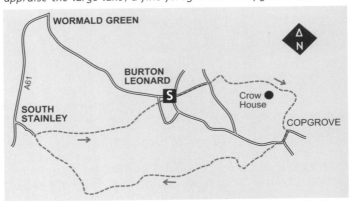

Your side branch, meanwhile, rises outside Dark Walk Wood, improves to a cart track and on to a bridle-gate onto the surfaced Green Lane. Turn right, soon reverting to a cart track, and the way drops to Robert Beck in the trees. Don't cross but take a left branch, which rises away slightly then runs a super course along fieldsides on the southern flank of the beck. A section midway is enclosed by hedgerows to eventually reach an access road to Lime Kilns Farm. Keep straight on, rising gently and largely surfaced to ultimately meet a T-junction. Turn right, dropping steadily to run to the edge of South Stainley. *En route you pass restored Stainley Hall; cross a stone-arched bridge on the beck, and conclude through a narrow wooded valley, with the old sandstone quarries of Stainley Gill.*

South Stainley is reached alongside St Wilfrid's church, with its bell-turret. *An old pump stands by the bridge, while two minutes further, at the A61, is the Red Lion pub and a roadside turnpike milestone.* Your route resumes by a stile on the right immediately before the church, and head past the churchyard to a stile/gate at the end. From here the return to Burton Leonard is largely a straight line. Continue along the hedgeside and on through a gateway in a hedge, continuing to a corner stile alongside a wood.

From a stile at the other end keep straight on with a hedge, a super green way that runs to meet a firm track coming in from the right. Keep straight on again for a considerable time, largely still with a hedgerow on your left. Ignore a branch left and advance on, dropping to cross a tiny stream in the bottom. Here the track swings right, but is soon left after reaching a hedge rising left. Here a more inviting grassy track ascends the fieldside to a gate into a replanted area. The track climbs steeply through infant trees then resumes on a hedgeside, with the village just ahead. Advance all the way to join a road, Scarah Lane. Turn left to emerge onto the top of the sloping High Green, descending back into the centre.

St Michael & All Angels, Copgrove

INDEX • *Walk number refers*

Agra Moor	15
Angram Reservoir	14
Azerley	20
Bewerley	5
Birstwith	2
Bishop Monkton	24
Bouthwaite	9,11
Bridge Hewick	23
Bridgehouse Gate	8
Brimham Rocks	4
Burn, River	15,17,19
Burnt Yates	1
Burton Leonard	25
Clint	1
Colsterdale	15
Copgrove	25
Dacre Banks	3
Dale Edge	10
Darley	3
Druid's Temple	16
Eavestone Lake	22
The Edge	13
Fearby	17
Fell Beck	4
Fountains Abbey	21
Fountains Earth Moor	9
Galphay	20
Glasshouses	6

Gollinglith Foot	15
Gouthwaite Res'r	7,9
Goyden Pot	13
Grewelthorpe	19
Guise Cliff	5
Hackfall Woods	19
Hampsthwaite	2
Hartwith	3
Heyshaw Moor	5
How Stean Gorge	12
Ilton	16
Ilton Moor	16
Kirkby Malzeard	20
Laver, River	20
Leighton	16
Leighton Reservoir	16
Littlethorpe	24
Lofthouse	11,12,13
Masham	17
Merryfield Mines	8
Mickley	18
Middlesmoor	10,12
Nidd, River	2,3,6,7,8,9
	10,11,13,14
North Stainley	18
Panorama Walk	6
Pateley Bridge	6,7,8

Ramsgill	9,11
Raven's Gill	5
Ripley	1
Ripon	23
Ripon Canal	24
Roundhill Reservoir	16
Sawley	22
Scar House Res'r	10,14
Scot Gate Ash Quarry	7
Shaw Mills	1
Skell, River	21,23
Sleningford Mill	18
Slipstone Crags	15
Smelthouses	4
South Stainley	25
Stean	12
Studley Roger	21
Studley Royal	21
Summerbridge	3
Swarcliffe	2
Thrope Edge	10
Ure, River	17,18
	19,23,24
Wath	7
West Tanfield	18
Winksley	20
Witton Moor	15
Yorke's Folly	5